Rock Climbing
The AMGA Single Pitch Manual

Bob Gaines and Jason D. Martin

GUILFORD, CONNECTICUT
HELENA, MONTANA

Copyright © 2014 by Bob Gaines and Jason D. Martin

FalconGuides is an imprint of Globe Pequot Press.
Falcon, FalconGuides, and Outfit Your Mind are registered trademarks of Rowman & Littlefield.

Photos: Bob Gaines unless credited otherwise.
Illustrations: Mike Clelland
Text and layout designer: Casey Shain
Project editor: Julie Marsh

Library of Congress Cataloging-in-Publication data is on file.

ISBN 978-0-7627-9004-3

Printed in the United States of America

Distributed by NATIONAL BOOK NETWORK

Contents

Chapter 1: The Role of a Climbing Instructor 1

Chapter 2: Professionalism

Chapter 3: Programming

Chapter 4: Pedagogy: The Art of Teaching

Chapter 5: Baseline Equipment

Chapter 6: Knots and Hitches

Chapter 7: Protection and Anchoring

Chapter 8: Anchor Systems

Chapter 9: Advanced Anchor Rigging Systems and Institutional Anchors

Chapter 10: Risk Management at the Crag

Chapter 11: Top- or Base-Site Management for a Single Pitch

Chapter 12: Rappelling

Chapter 13: Basic Assistance and Rescue Skills

Chapter 14: Fixed Lines

Chapter 15: Leading

Acknowledgments

The creation of a book like this is a grand effort with many parties involved. First, we would like to thank those who assisted the most in this process: Ron Funderburke and Ed Crothers of the AMGA, and John Burbidge and Julie Marsh from Globe Pequot Press. Ed and Ron provided most of the technical support for this text from the AMGA, and John and Julie patiently worked to put it all together. Special thanks to Casey Shain for the excellent job on the layout and design.

Thanks to the instructors, guides, and volunteers who took time out of their busy schedules to pose for, shoot, and donate photos for this project. In particular, Bob would like to thank Patty Kline, Mark O'Brien, Erik Kramer-Webb, Tony Grice, Dave Mayville, Ryan Murphy, Reggie Bulman, Kevin Jackson, Bryan Baez, Robin Depke, Ryan Bennet, William Jaques, Adam Radford, Wills Young, Nicholas Giblin, Chris Idiart, Dan Richter, Frank Bentwood, Terri Condon, David Berlin, Ben Shackelford, Andrew Jones, Eric Ludwig, Adam Hufford, Kris Jackson, Todd Gordon, and Chris Ramirez. Jason would like to thank Tim Page, James Pierson, Richard Riquleme, Jeremy Wilson, and Betsy Winter. We would also like to thank those who gave us feedback throughout this process. These include John Belanger, Tom Kirby, Casey O'Brien, and Dunham Gooding.

Thanks to our fellow guides and mentors who have taught us so much over the years. Jason would like to specifically thank Michael Powers, Art Mooney, Tom Hargis, Marcus Jollif, and Adam Fox. Bob would like to thank Jon Tierney, Alan Jolley, Peter Croft, Scott Cosgrove, Marcus Jollif, Dylan Taylor, Josh Jackson, Chris Baumann, Todd Vogel, Erik Kramer-Webb, Tony Grice, Tony Sartin, Pat Dennis, and Dave Mayville. Bob would like to give a sincere thanks to John Long for the many insightful conversations while working together on the Climbing Anchors books.

And finally, we would like to thank our families. Jason would like to thank Krista, Holly, and Caden for supporting all of his endeavors. And Bob would like to thank his wife, Yvonne, for her help with the photography.

Introduction

Rock climbing is a sport unlike any other. Hanging on by your fingertips, high above the ground, gives us a sense of focus and freedom that few other activities provide. We love the feeling of the warm sun on our backs while we stick the perfect jam or pull the crux move. We relish in our movement over the stone and the beauty of our surroundings. We love the element of exploration that comes with the sport and the anticipation of a trip to a new crag or the ascent of a new route. And we adore both the acquaintances that are made on the rock as well as the enduring friendships that are built within a climbing partnership.

We love it all so much that we have a desire to share it with others.

And while we wish to share this with others, we have to understand that the role of the climbing instructor comes with a great deal of responsibility. People can get hurt or even killed in this sport. With that in mind, it's important that those who wish to teach have the proper training before instructing any level of climber.

This text was designed to be a supplement to the American Mountain Guides Association Single Pitch Instructor (SPI) Course. The SPI course was designed to help capable recreational climbers transition into capable and effective climbing instructors. The course—and this text—focuses on the technical skills required of an instructor as they are applied in all forms of single pitch climbing instruction. In addition to this, the course addresses the essential educational and environmental tenets required to teach climbing. AMGA Single Pitch Instructors are expected to demonstrate the technical and educational proficiencies necessary to instruct a variety of single pitch rock climbing skills in a secure and effective manner to both groups and individuals.

The SPI course is intended for recreational climbers who are already proficient in both toprope and lead climbing. It was designed to benefit those who wish to facilitate outdoor climbing programs for groups such as those offered by guide services, camps, schools, universities, climbing clubs, therapeutic groups, churches, and climbing gyms.

Those who wish to teach climbing in the outdoors tend to have a higher success rate obtaining employment as climbing instructors with this training and certification. Additionally, the AMGA recommends this program as a precursor to upper-level AMGA climbing instruction and guide programs.

About the American Mountain Guides Association (AMGA)

The American Mountain Guides Association is the organization that oversees guide and instructor training in the United States, while also supporting and advocating for climbing instructors, guides, and accredited guide services. The organization is dedicated to supporting these groups through excellence in instructor and guide education, through the development of standards to ensure the quality of services provided to the public, and by serving as a resource for access to and the protection of the natural environment. As a group, the AMGA

AMGA presidents at the 2010 AMGA annual meeting. Back row, from left to right: Alan Pietrasanta, Ian Wade, John Cleary, Mark Houston, Dunham Gooding, Phil Powers, Dick Jackson, and John Bicknell. Front row, kneeling: Margaret Wheeler and Doug Robinson.

BETSY WINTER

presents a strong and unified voice for high standards of professionalism in guiding and climbing instruction.

The AMGA is grounded in a powerful tradition that continues to evolve with the ever-changing arena of mountain guiding and climbing instruction. The organization offers a series of training courses and exams designed to certify guides and climbing instructors to highly respected and internationally recognized standards.

A Brief History of the AMGA

The profession of instructing and guiding in the mountains spans back to the start of the United States as a nation. However, it wasn't until 1979 that a group of twelve guides got together in Jackson, Wyoming, and decided that it was time to formalize an organization to represent the greater guiding community. The goals these guides developed were written in a bar on the back of a napkin and became known as the Moose Bar Charter. As a result, the American Professional Mountain Guides Association was born. Over the next few years, the "P" was dropped, and the AMGA developed and grew throughout the United States.

In the AMGA's formative years, there was a great deal of wrangling. Instructors and guides are independent minded, and an organization overseeing standards wasn't always popular. Early presidents such as Doug Robinson, Alan Pietrasanta, Ian Wade, and Dunham Gooding spent much of their time trying to expand the ranks of the guides involved, while also overseeing the development of certification courses for guides and accreditation programs for guide services.

Unity among guides and guide services became especially important in the mid-1980s. At that time a worldwide liability insurance crisis shook the guiding industry to its core. After steps were taken to secure affordable insurance appropriate for climbing schools and guide services, independent-minded guides began to see that there was great value in working together as an association.

The next major goal of the AMGA was to gain acceptance into the International Federation of Mountain Guides Associations (IFMGA). Admission into this organization would allow American guides access to the European Alps while recognizing that AMGA programs met an international standard. Between 1990 and 1997, AMGA presidents Steve Young, Dunham Gooding, Matt Culbertson, and John Cleary worked tirelessly to achieve this goal. On November 22, 1997, delegates admitted the AMGA into the IFMGA after a unanimous vote from the existing member countries. Today the AMGA is the sole representative of the United States to the twenty-six-member IFMGA, the international governing body responsible for guiding standards and education around the world.

In the late 1990s, under the supervision of Mark Houston, both as technical director and then as president, and with help from Jon Tierney and others, the AMGA developed the Toprope Site

Manager program. Unfortunately, the TRSM program was limited in its scope and didn't adequately meet the needs of instructors looking to advance to higher-level AMGA courses. It wasn't until 2008, under the supervision of Adam Fox, that the Single Pitch Instructor program became the nation's premier entry-level program for those who sought to be climbing instructors. In 2009, after a third party review, the AMGA SPI received the endorsement of the UIAA (Union Internationale des Associations d'Alpinisme) as meeting the international standards for the training of climbing instructors.

Today the AMGA continues to develop its programs to meet changing standards and to support the growing community of guides and climbing instructors in the United States. In addition, the organization has become a resource for land managers and outdoor industry leaders by promoting land stewardship, world-class training, and sustainable practices to protect our natural resources.

The AMGA is the post-graduate school of guiding, and it is where professional climbing instructors and guides go to develop their skills in order to attain the highest level of training and certification.

AMGA Certification

There are three disciplines of certification in the AMGA: Rock, Alpine, and Ski. Some of the disciplines have multiple levels of certification. For example, in the Rock discipline one can be certified at the Single Pitch Instructor level, the Rock Instructor level, or the Rock Guide level. In each of the disciplines, the guide level is the highest level of certification. If an individual obtains AMGA certification at the guide level in Rock, Alpine, and Ski, then that person will be granted the International Federation of Mountain Guides Associations (IFMGA) certification, which is the highest level of certification available for a guide.

The Single Pitch Instructor certification was designed for those who wish to work in a single pitch setting and as an entry-level program for those who wish to continue on to gain a higher level of training and certification.

If you are interested in working solely in a single pitch setting, then there is no reason to continue on to a higher level of training. However, if you do wish to work on multi-pitch rock terrain, in the alpine, or on skis, then additional courses will be required in order for you to be adequately trained.

Following is a breakdown of the different types of certification available from the AMGA and the terrain guidelines for the certifications:

AMGA Single Pitch Instructor

AMGA Single Pitch Instructors are trained and assessed to operate on all routes that:

- The anchors are accessed by either nontechnical terrain or by leading technical 5th-class terrain.
- Are climbed without intermediate belays.
- Present no difficulties on approach or retreat from the area, such as routefinding, scrambling, or navigating.

AMGA Climbing Wall Instructor—Toprope

AMGA Climbing Wall Instructors (Toprope) are trained and assessed to operate on indoor climbing and bouldering walls and climbing structures that:

- Do not involve lead climbing.
- Do not include the instruction of lead climbing.

AMGA Climbing Wall Instructor—Lead

AMGA Climbing Wall Instructors (Lead) are trained and assessed to operate on indoor climbing and bouldering walls and climbing structures that:

- Involve lead climbing.
- Include the instruction of lead climbing.

AMGA Rock Instructor

Rock Instructor certification is designed to apply to most "cragging" rock climbing areas in the United States. AMGA Rock Instructors are trained and assessed to operate on all rock routes that:

- Are Yosemite Decimal System Grade III or shorter in length.
- Do not have approaches or descents where extensive use of short-rope techniques is appropriate for security.
- Are not remote in nature.
- Do not involve technical snow, glacier travel, the use of skis, or exposure to avalanche risk.

AMGA Rock Guide

Rock Guide certification is designed to apply to all Rock Instructor terrain, but it also includes climbs of much greater length, including big wall and aid climbs, and climbs where significant short-roping is appropriate for the safeguarding of clients on either approaches or descents. AMGA Rock Guide certification is not, however, applicable to terrain that is alpine in nature (i.e., remote or involves technical snow or technical glaciated or icy terrain). AMGA Rock Guides are trained and assessed to operate on all rock routes that:

- Are Yosemite Decimal System Grade IV or Grade V in length.
- Include approaches and descents that may require extensive use of short-roping technique for security.
- May be remote in nature.
- Do not involve glacier travel, the use of skis, or exposure to avalanche risk.

AMGA Alpine Guide

AMGA Alpine Guide certification is designed for guiding glaciated and non-glaciated peaks, approaches, and climbs, with no limitation with respect to season or elevation. It includes rock climbs, peak ascents, waterfall ice climbs, and expeditionary climbing. AMGA Alpine Guides are trained and assessed to operate in all alpine and rock terrains that:

- Are Yosemite Decimal System Grade V or shorter (for rock routes).

- Are not conducted on skis where the main objective of the outing is either a ski tour or the enjoyment of downhill skiing.

- AMGA Alpine Guides who hold both Alpine and Rock Guide certifications are allowed to guide alpine rock routes that are YDS Grade V or longer.

AMGA Ski Guide

AMGA Ski Guide certification is designed for guiding either ski tours or ski ascents/descents on alpine touring or free-heel equipment. AMGA Certified Ski Guides are trained and assessed to operate in all terrains that:

- Include as the main objective either ski touring, off-piste, and/or mechanized skiing.

- Are on slopes up to 50 degrees.

- May employ the use of rope including short-roping techniques with the use of ice axe and crampons.

- Require travel on crevassed glaciers.

- Have significant avalanche hazard.

- Involve multi-pitch ice or rock.

IFMGA American Mountain Guide

IFMGA American Mountain Guide certification is designed for individuals certified as AMGA Rock, Alpine, and Ski Guides. IFMGA/American Mountain Guides are trained and assessed to operate in all alpine, rock, and ski terrain.

Concept Driven Techniques and the AMGA

"I want to learn the AMGA way."

The preceding comment is incredibly common. But it is a misperception of what the AMGA is and what it does. There is no "AMGA way."

The American Mountain Guides Association teaches students a series of different techniques in each of the disciplines. Association guidelines seldom dictate which technique an individual is required to use. Instead, AMGA program instructors evaluate their students on the application of the techniques that they have learned. In other words, one student might accomplish the exact same goal using a completely different technique than another student, but both might still be acceptable.

There are a lot of right ways to do things. Some ways may be more efficient and some ways may be more effective. The goal of an AMGA instructor is to find the best and most efficient way based on the circumstance.

In the Single Pitch Instructor curriculum, there are a handful of prescribed techniques that are taught. However, the bulk of the material is driven by concept. A concept is a general idea of how something should work. For example, you may wish to set up a toprope with an anchor that self-adjusts to a variable direction of load. There are a number of ways to do this. You could use a quad or a magic-x with load limiting knots, or an equalette. What you use doesn't matter. Instead, what matters is that you achieved a self-adjusting system, which is conceptual in nature.

In the SPI curriculum there are a number of concepts. An SPI provider's goal is not necessarily to have a student ape exactly what is in this text, or exactly what an individual instructor has taught, but instead to demonstrate an understanding of each concept and how to apply it.

How to Use This Book

This book is broken into two major sections. The first part (chapters 1 through 4) covers instructor knowledge. The information here, concerning everything from professionalism to pedagogy, combines to provide a foundation of base-level knowledge that every climbing instructor should have. The second part (chapters 5 through 15) delves into the specific technical skills that are needed to effectively run programs in a single pitch setting.

Like the first part, this second part also provides a foundation, though this foundation is built of technical skills.

To fully understand and appreciate the material presented in this text, readers should have a solid understanding of toproped climbing and have experience with traditional climbing. This is not a "how-to-toprope" book or a "how-to-lead-climb" book, but a book that assumes you already have those skills and wish to take them to the next level.

This text was specifically designed as a supplement to the AMGA SPI program. It was not designed to be used by independent practitioners without the oversight of a qualified instructor. Readers of this book are strongly advised to work through the material herein with an AMGA Single Pitch Instructor Program Provider.

A student topropes a climb at Joshua Tree National Park, California.

JASON D. MARTIN

CHAPTER 1

The Role of a Climbing Instructor

Working as a climbing instructor is a very special job. The dream is alluring: work at the crag every day under cloudless skies, become a master climber, explore new places, meet fascinating people, and teach them the art of rock craft. And while the dream is alluring, it doesn't reflect the complete picture. The reality is that when you become a climbing instructor you are no longer able to follow your climbing whims or operate the way you may have in the past as a recreational climber.

Working as a climbing instructor and climbing recreationally are two very different things. Recreational climbers assume a limited amount of responsibility for one another. There is an implied assumption between partners that each person will be the primary manager of his or her own safety.

Professional climbing instructors are not climbing recreationally and are not climbing for themselves. The job requires managing risk first, followed closely by the quality of the student experience.

The most critical role that a climbing instructor provides is that of a risk manager. First, we have to manage our own exposure to the inherent risks of working in a vertical environment. There is no student security without instructor security. And second, we must manage the risk to our students.

While risk management is the most important aspect of the climbing instructor's job, the quality of the student experience comes in a close second.

When working in a climbing program, personal goals and ambitions are put aside. It is not about you "living the dream," but instead is about the students, their goals, and their ambitions.

At the outset one of the best ways to achieve the dual objectives of managing risk and student experience is to choose an appropriate crag. If the crag is appropriate to the student(s), then both the objective and subjective dangers will be manageable. Additionally, the student climber will feel comfortable in the setting and will be more emotionally open to learning the art of climbing.

The other major difference between recreational climbing and climbing instruction is the obvious fact that a climbing program is an instructional setting where students look for advice and training. This means, for example, that once an appropriate crag has been chosen, then the next step is to choose an appropriate curriculum. Think about where a student is at the beginning of the day, and what the desired goal is at the end. Don't skip or rush through instruction to accommodate instructor desires. Focus on where the student is and where he or she needs to be.

The most effective instructors are those who recognize these distinctions early in their instructional career. The most ineffective are those who attempt to teach while still acting as a recreational climber.

Terri Condon leads a trad climb during her AMGA Single Pitch Instructor Assessment at Joshua Tree National Park, California.

CHAPTER 2

Professionalism

Doctors, lawyers, and teachers don't have too many conversations about professionalism. They don't have to. They act the part without anybody telling them to. They dress appropriately for their workday, they use the language of their respective professions, they make concrete plans about how they are going to handle the challenges of their day, and they are respectful of those they're working with. Additionally, professionals are up to date with the best and most current practices in their field, they undergo formal training, they demonstrate a level of mastery through peer assessment and certification, they pursue continuing education, and they adhere to a code of ethics.

When climbing instructors act professionally, they represent three different interests. First, they represent themselves. If an instructor would like to be thought of as a respected professional, then she has to act as one. Second, they represent the companies, schools, or programs that they work for. In this day and age, a lack of professionalism can lead to negative press online, which can have a serious and long-term impact. And third, instructors represent all climbing instructors. If a recreational climber has a negative experience with one climbing instructor, that often creates an impression of climbing instructors in general.

Clearly, if an instructor develops a reputation for a lack of professionalism, it will affect his or her bottom line. Program directors don't want to hear anything negative about their instructors. What they want to hear is that everybody had a successful and enjoyable day.

Presenting oneself as a professional engenders trust and confidence from one's students. But there's a great deal more to professionalism than just attitude. Professionalism is something that should permeate every instructional day from the moment a student has contact with an organization to the moment he or she leaves.

Pre-Program Preparations

Professionalism starts in the office. The best way to present a professional program is to be prepared. Following is a short list of questions to consider before meeting students at the crag:

- Are there land-use permits in place or has permission to operate at the location been granted? If charging for a program on public lands, a land-use permit will be required. If operating on private lands, you may need to obtain permission.

- What are the rules and regulations regarding the area?

- Do you have liability insurance, or do you have coverage from the organization that you're working for?

- Do the marketing materials accurately reflect the experience that you will provide your students?

- If working a course for an organization, do you know what the marketing materials say about the course or program that you intend to run?

- Do the students have any medical conditions?

- Do you have student emergency contact information?

- Did you collect climbing biographies from your students?

- Have you or a representative from your organization been made available to the students to answer any questions that they might have?

- Have you researched the area where you plan to operate? Do you have a Plan B, in case your initial plan for the day falls through due to crowding or some other unforeseen circumstance?

- If it's going to be an instructional day, do you have lessons prepared?

- Do you have a release or acknowledgement of risk form for your students?

- Have you developed an emergency plan?

- Do you have appropriate first-aid training for the location that you intend to work?

- Do you have other required credentials? Some areas require instructors to obtain a state guide's license, and others require individuals to hold a Leave No Trace Trainer or Master Educator certification. If you're providing meals, some areas may require that you hold a food handler's license.

Obviously, some of these issues will be the responsibility of the organization an instructor works for. However, if the organization doesn't provide information on the questions that seem to be its responsibility, then it's the instructor's responsibility to make sure that each of these questions has been answered.

At the Instructional Site

Professionalism continues from the office and into the field. Once in the field, an instructor is a role model not only for the students, but also for other recreational climbers in the area. With that in mind, instructors should model the way that they believe people should act at the crag by being considerate and having a low impact.

Managing both the students and the scene is an important part of the day. This management doesn't necessarily relate only to the technical and pedagogical aspects, but it also pertains to how the instructor relates to the group, how the group acts, and how the instructor interacts with recreational climbers.

The crag needs to be a place for people to experience climbing without feeling put down or threatened. Threatening language in particular is sometimes not obvious and can come from inappropriate comments or jokes that might seem minor to an instructor, but can have an impact on one or more of the students. It is important to continually monitor the language, jokes, and conversations taking place so that all members feel respected.

When in contact with recreational climbers or other instructors, be professional, courteous, and friendly. Try not to tie up routes when other parties are waiting and make sure that students park themselves and their gear in unobtrusive places.

The ropes, harnesses, and equipment used on a program should be in good repair. The instructor's rack and rope should be organized in the instructor's pack before arriving at the crag. When unpacked, everything should remain organized. Avoid creating a "yard sale" at the base of the crag with equipment and packs scattered all over the place.

Most instructors choose to carry a notebook with student information, lesson plans, and time management strategies. This helps an instructor stay on track and organized. An organically run day without set lessons, strategies, and notes is feasible for advanced-level instructors, but should be avoided by those new to the profession.

The way that each individual instructs is different, and it's often difficult to determine how long it will take to teach certain lessons or to cycle through students at a toprope or rappel site. For new instructors it's important to keep track of how long each activity takes in the instructor's notebook. This will help with time management strategies on future programs.

Managing student time is only one aspect of time management. Often the most time-consuming element of the day is setting up and taking down systems. It is imperative that instructors have mastery of these foundational skills. Additionally, when planning for the day, instructors need to remember to account for this time.

AMGA Single Pitch Instructors are required to be able to lead 5.6 traditional routes and to toprope 5.8, both in good style. These are minimum standards, and most instructors climb harder than the standard. Though an ability to "climb hard" is not a prerequisite for an instructor, an ability to model good technique is. Professional instructors should constantly work on their climbing skills in order to demonstrate the best technique possible.

Professionalism at the crag is essential. A climbing instructor's professional demeanor should be a model for students, for recreational climbers, and for other instructors from before the trip starts to the moment that the last student leaves.

A stack of permits and permit applications at the American Alpine Institute.

JASON D. MARTIN

CHAPTER 3

Programming

Most climbing schools offer a variety of courses. Within the simple beginner to advanced-level framework, there might be any number of courses that focus on a specific skill or a specific series of skills. These could include anything from beginner courses for people who have never put on a harness before, to advanced courses in high-end movement or traditional lead climbing.

Regardless of the course, the one thing that instructors must keep in mind is that students signed up for a specific curriculum, and aside from managing risk, the most important instructor goal of the day should be to honor that curriculum.

To provide the curriculum that has been sold, instructors will need to find an appropriate crag for the program. To operate at the crag, they will need a land-use permit and an understanding of liability. They will need to be aware of risk management issues and develop an emergency response plan. They should be conscious of crag etiquette and advocacy. And they will need to have functional equipment for their programs and foster good communication with other staff members. In other words, to provide the curriculum that has been sold, the instructor will have to do a lot of prep work.

Permitting

In the United States, climbing destinations are managed by a patchwork of different agencies that operate independently of one another. On the federal level the primary land managers include the National Park Service, the USDA Forest Service, and the Bureau of Land Management. Regional land managers include state, county, and city parks and private lands. This variety and the many different and sometimes contradictory rules and regulations pose serious administrative challenges. In addition to all this, the resource is not growing, but the demands on the resource are.

The popularity of recreation on public lands has exploded over the last decade. This has resulted in more and more commercial operators vying for a limited number of permits. The combination of this and the mandate that land managers preserve and protect wild places has created an often-frustrating challenge for independent instructors and organizations that seek land-use permits.

Legal access to public lands in particular is important because most climbing instruction takes place on such lands. If the students pay a fee of any sort to participate—whether for a commercial operation, a nonprofit, an individual instructor, a school, or a university—then a permit is required to operate legally on public lands.

Operating on public lands without a permit is breaking the law and could result in a wide array of consequences. These range from a minor citation to a significant fine or even an arrest. In some cases it is possible to be permanently banned from public lands for willfully disregarding land-use regulations. Indeed, there are some insurance providers that will deny coverage if they discover that an operator was working without a permit at the time of an incident that resulted in a lawsuit. Working on public lands without a permit is serious and should never be taken lightly.

There are two main questions that an individual or an organization should ask to determine whether or not a land-use permit is required:

(1) Did the participants pay to engage in the activity?

Did they pay any fee at all? Were they asked to pay tuition for the course or guided days? Were they asked to submit a donation to the program? Are they required to rent equipment from the operation in order to participate?

If the answer to any of these questions is yes, then the land manager should be contacted to determine if a commercial-use permit is required. Even if you are a volunteer instructor for a club, but the club is taking in funds, the land manager should be contacted to determine if a permit is required.

(2) Are the instructors getting paid to run the program or to provide the instruction?

If the instructors receive any kind of compensation, then they or the organization will need to obtain a permit. Compensation could mean an hourly or daily wage, a stipend, meals, or even "free" equipment. Nearly any type of compensation outside of a thank-you constitutes commercial use.

There is a bit of a gray area when it comes to salaried teachers or professors who work with students from their school at a crag. Some land managers will require such a group to obtain a permit, whereas others will allow it to operate without one. Teachers and professors should contact the land manager at the desired location for more information.

Some public lands have special permits for educational institutions and not-for-profits. Educators are encouraged to contact land managers to see if they have programs like this available. If an area does not offer "educational permits," it is encouraged to suggest such a program to the manager.

The first step to obtaining use authorization is to contact the land management agency and get in touch with the person who handles recreational commercial or nonprofit use.

If the land manager is accepting new permit holders, he or she will provide an application. It is not uncommon for the application process to take a significant amount of time, so plan adequately.

Nearly all permit applications will require some kind of application fee. It is not uncommon for land managers to also ask for additional monies prior to the issuance of a permit. These include, but are not limited to, monitoring fees, reservation fees, or administrative fees. The costs for all of these vary based on the land management agency and the type of permit.

Nearly every land manager will require commercial users to hold general liability insurance before issuing a permit. The land manager is usually included in the policy as an "additional insured." This liability policy—often between $500,000 and $1,000,000—provides them some cover if an accident takes place during a program.

At the end of the year, the permit holder will be required to submit reports that include revenues and user days. Many contracts include a clause that states that the land manager has the right to audit a permit holder at any time. Therefore it is important for organizations to keep excellent financial and user day records, as failure to do so could lead to the loss of the permit. It should be noted that many land managers compare your reports to any other reports that they have on hand. For example, if an instructor has to sign in at a ranger station before operating each day, the land manager will compare the final report to the information gathered at the station.

Fees are calculated in different ways. Some land managers charge a flat fee for operations, whereas others charge anywhere from 2 percent to 4.5 percent of gross income. Most charge 3 percent of gross.

Guides, instructors, and guide services spend a great deal of time trying to obtain and then maintain their permits. For many, this is a major administrative duty. As a result, the way that the majority of new guides and instructors choose to access public or private lands is through guide services or other organizations that have laid the groundwork and developed relationships with local land managers. In many cases it is much easier to get hired by a guide service than it is to obtain an individual permit.

Risk Management and Liability

In the context of climbing instruction, risk management is broadly defined as the identification of the risks that pose a threat to students, instructors, or a program, and to find ways to avoid or mitigate those risks.

A recommended practice for avoiding and mitigating risk is to systematically assess potential sources of harm, outline ways to avoid or reduce exposure to harm, and determine how to respond in the event of an incident or accident. When compiled into a document, a risk management plan is created. No matter the size of the program, from the very smallest to the very largest, the development of a written plan is essential. Additionally, everyone involved with the program should have a copy of the plan and be familiar with the contents.

An intelligent and well thought out risk management plan accomplishes the following:

- It can greatly reduce the number and severity of incidents or injuries.
- It protects the instructor and the program from potential negligence lawsuits.
- In the event of a negligence lawsuit, it can provide a layer of protection to the instructor and program during the defense against the suit.

An emergency response plan is typically a part of the overall risk management plan.

There are a number of considerations that should be addressed in the plan.

First-Aid Requirements

Climbing instructors must have appropriate first-aid training. The AMGA terrain standards state that Single Pitch Instructors are required to hold and maintain a Wilderness First Aid (WFA) certificate if they intend to work in the frontcountry, or a Wilderness First Responder (WFR) certificate if they intend to work in the backcountry. If it will take less than 2 hours to evacuate a student to definitive medical care, then an instructor is working in the frontcountry. However, if it will take more than 2 hours, then an instructor is working in the backcountry and will need to hold a WFR certification. Additionally, instructors must hold a CPR certification. Most American guide services require their instructors to maintain WFR and CPR certifications.

Participant Screening

Collect both physical and medical information on the trip's participants. Be sure to be aware of any conditions that might need to be considered before the trip, such as allergies, injuries, or medical conditions that could hinder a student's ability to participate. It is important to have this information in the field in case something happens, but it is equally important to protect each student's privacy in these matters.

Communications

If an incident occurs, it is imperative to have a communications plan. If the plan is to use a cell phone for this, be sure to know where there is reception and to have all appropriate phone numbers. If using a radio, a sat phone, or a personal locator beacon, understand how each of the devices work. Additionally, if there is a possibility that students will be required to operate one of these devices, they will need to be briefed on their use.

Evacuation

Instructors need to have a plan for an injured climber. Obviously there are levels of injury—some will only require an easy hike out, whereas others may involve a carryout or even an air evacuation. If evacuating the climber, an instructor should know where the nearest hospital is located. If calling for a rescue, have an understanding of what will happen and who will show up.

Minors

In the United States, by law, a minor child cannot enter into a contractual agreement. A release of liability is a contract. Additionally, some states allow legal guardians of minor children to sign away their right to sue; most do not. There are strategies for dealing with this dilemma, but they are beyond the scope of this book. The bottom line for the Single Pitch Instructor is to be aware of the protocols put in place by the organization one works for and to follow those protocols.

Student Safety Briefing

Before the trip starts, explain safety procedures to your students. Brief them on the communications plan and where the nearest hospital is located. If carpooling to the crag, it will be important for everyone to note where the keys are stored, whether in a pack, a pocket, or hidden near the vehicle. And lastly, the instructor should show the students where he or she keeps the first-aid kit and check to see who else in the group has first-aid training.

Post-Trip Contact

Establish somebody to check in with at the end of each program. If the instructor does not check in on time, that person needs to have instructions on what he or she should do to facilitate a rescue.

Incident Debrief

If something happens and a student or an instructor is hurt, or if there is a "close call," it's important to debrief the incident with the organization's management and with other instructors. Climbing instructors can learn a great deal from discussions following an incident.

Assumption of Risk and Liability Release Forms

Another important risk management tool is the use of release of liability or assumption of risk forms. When well crafted, these documents serve two purposes. First, they inform participants of the "inherent risks" that are or could be involved in rock climbing. Even the best risk management planning cannot eliminate all risk. Inherent risks are risks that are an integral part of an activity, which, if removed, completely alter the nature of the activity. By signing one of these documents, a participant is acknowledging that they have been made aware of the risks and that they are choosing to participate despite the risks.

Second, in the event of a participant's injury or death, these documents protect the instructor and program from charges of negligence. Simply put, negligence means that the instructor and the program have a "duty" to manage the "foreseeable" risk of harm to participants. A claim of negligence means that they failed in that duty, an incident occurred, and the participant suffered a loss. With a properly executed release of liability form, a participant is agreeing to give up the right to sue for negligence.

It is essential that all participants sign a release of liability or an assumption of risk form. Making sure that happens is often the responsibility of the climbing instructor. A recommended procedure for executing this process properly is to:

- Inform participants to read and, if they agree to the terms, sign and date the document.

- Allow the participants time to read the document. This process should not be rushed.

- Collect the documents, making sure they have not been altered and are signed and dated. If the form uses boxes or lines after paragraphs, be sure they are checked or initialed.

- Store in a secure location.

If a participant will not sign the document as it is written, they cannot be allowed to participate in the activity. Also, it is not the responsibility of the instructor to interpret language in the document for participants. A well-written release should use language that a "reasonable" person can understand. If the same questions come up time and again, it is time to have the document reviewed by an attorney familiar with recreation law.

Liability

A question often asked by climbing instructors is "Can I be held personally liable and sued in the event of an accident?"

The bad news is that the answer is yes. If an accident involving serious injury or the death of a participant occurs, a lawsuit may follow. Along with the program, it is common that the instructor involved will be named as a defendant. The good news is that having general liability insurance will assist in the defense of the suit, and if a settlement is either reached between the parties or is handed down by the court, it will cover all or most of the settlement costs and, in some cases, but not all, attorney fees. That said, it is important to understand that not all liability insurance policies are created equally. These types of policies tend to be written in technical language that is difficult for the layperson to understand, consist of many pages, include exclusions, and don't make for the most exciting reading. Regardless, there are several questions a climbing instructor should ask:

- Are all employees covered? This may depend on whether the instructor is an employee or an independent contractor.

- Does it cover all activities? For example, some policies will cover rock climbing, but not ice climbing.

- Is it in effect for all areas of operation? The policy may not be in effect if the instructor or program is guiding without a permit.

For the climbing instructor, the name of the game is to reduce exposure to liability. Basically, this means conducting business at the "standard of a reasonable professional." This includes, but is not limited to, following a program's policies and procedures, being in step with current industry standards, using appropriate and well-maintained equipment, being respectful and building a good rapport with students, adhering to the rules and regulations of land management agencies, and getting training and, ideally, certification for the terrain worked on.

Even when following the best practices, there are a couple of subtle ways that climbing instructors can inadvertently increase their exposure to liability. The first is misrepresentation. An example of this would be an instructor who markets services as an "AMGA Guide," "trained and certified by the AMGA," or any of a number of other examples, but in reality is an AMGA Single Pitch Instructor. The problem here is that it would be pretty easy for a participant to make the case that when he purchased the services of an "AMGA Guide," he thought was hiring a fully certified IFMGA/AMGA Guide; in other words, he paid for one thing and got something else. In legal terms, this is referred to as "fraudulent inducement." If a court were to uphold the accusation, one likely outcome would be that all contracts between the instructor and the participant would be nullified; this includes the release of liability. Should that occur in a negligence suit, one of the most important tools for the defense is gone. The solution to this problem is easy: Instructors need to be specific about who they are and what they do when promoting their services.

The other subtle way to increase exposure to liability is to tell participants they will be kept safe. A legal definition of the word *safe* is "free from harm." As mentioned earlier, a "reasonable person" understands or has been informed that there are inherent risks in rock climbing. However, if marketing materials, operations manuals, a website, or the instructor tell participants that they will be kept safe and someone is injured or killed, any defense that might have been provided by the common law doctrine of inherent risk will have been severely compromised, if not lost. Again, the solution is fairly simple: Climbing is not safe, don't say that it is.

Risk Management in the Field

For AMGA Single Pitch Instructors, there are four types of risk that students might encounter on a program. They are psychological, sociological, financial, and physical. It's important to recognize each of these risks to students and to understand how to mitigate them.

Psychological

The fear of falling and the fear of heights are simultaneously attractive and repellent to students. Many new climbers are fascinated by the idea that they can climb to a point where a fall would result in their death, whereas others seek out climbing to combat a fear of heights.

There are two common ways to alleviate a student's fear of heights. The first is to spend a significant amount of time early in the day discussing "the system." In other words, explain the strengths of the ropes, the slings, and the other equipment. The idea is to assure students intellectually that the system will not fail. The problem is that an intellectual discussion is often not enough to alleviate the emotional nature of their fears.

The second way is through exposure therapy. The more often a climber is lowered on a climbing rope and caught by a belay, the more secure he will

feel. Additionally, the more that a climber actually climbs, the more secure he will feel. For this reason, it's always a good idea to have a beginner climb a route more than once.

In extreme situations where a climber has a severe fear of heights, instructors might consider using incremental exposure therapy. In other words, have the student climb up 5 feet and then lower him. Then have the student climb up 8 feet and lower again. Every time the climber goes up, there will be an incremental decrease in fear. This is because the climber is becoming familiar with both the moves on the route and the security offered by the system.

Sociological

A second risk is fear of failure in front of other students, or in front of the instructor. Some may even be afraid of ridicule for their failure. It's not uncommon for students to apologize for their inability to complete a route. Some are embarrassed, and others believe that the fact they didn't get up somehow damaged the day for other students or the instructor. This, of course, couldn't be further from the truth.

Students need to be comfortable with you and with the others in your program. Instructors should strive to create a place where it is acceptable for their students to fail. At times this may mean moderating student comments to ensure that negativity is kept to a minimum.

Another excellent tool is for the students to see the instructor challenged on a route. Once a student has displayed competency with belaying, climb a route that is hard for you and let the students watch as you try to work out the moves. This will help them to understand that working a route, taking falls, and failing is part of the game.

Financial

Anytime a person spends money on a program, there is financial risk. A lot can go wrong that could make an individual feel like she wasted her money. These include the following:

A professional search and rescue deputy is short-hauled to an accident victim in Red Rock Canyon, Nevada.

JASON D. MARTIN

- Program goals were not met.
- Course was poorly or unprofessionally run.
- Student was placed in a course that didn't match her skill level.
- Personal equipment is lost or broken.

These four financial risks are easily averted. First and foremost, it's important to run a professional program. Instructors should meet and attempt to exceed all program goals.

Second, when screening someone for a program, ask probing questions to make sure that the student is placed in the proper course. Occasionally an instructor is placed in the awkward position of working with a student who has been assigned to the wrong program. A skilled instructor does her best to accommodate the person, and then makes sure that program administrators are made aware of the mistake.

And finally, be careful with student gear. Make sure that everyone leaves with the same equipment they arrived with.

Physical

The most obvious risk in rock climbing is that of an injury or a fatality. This is likely the number one risk that students think about when they sign up for a course.

The best instructors are those that are a little bit paranoid. Managing risk is paramount in climbing instruction, and an instructor who can imagine a wide array of dangers is an instructor who is likely to keep her students from injury.

There are a handful of things a climbing instructor can do to mitigate physical risk:

- Orient students to safety procedures around the crag. These include everything from checking knots to belay backups to climbing commands, etc.
- Create boundaries at the climbing site. Some crags are exposed, and there are places where students shouldn't be without a rope. Other crags may have excellent resting spots where

students can relax away from the base without their helmets on. Make it clear to students what is appropriate at the crag.

- If working with other instructors, meet regularly to discuss risks and other programming issues. If working alone, set aside time to speak to other instructors and program administrators about their experiences.

Risk management and liability in adventure sports and adventure tourism is a massive subject. Seminars are held every year on this topic at the Association for Outdoor Recreation and Education (AORE) Conference, at the Wilderness Risk Management Conference, and at the Association for Experiential Education (AEE) Conference. Additionally, dozens of books, blogs, and websites are devoted to the subject.

Understanding liability is something that instructors—especially independent instructors—need to invest themselves in just as deeply as the rest of their training. Knowledge of liability issues is not the sexiest part of the climbing world, but can go a long way toward keeping an instructor in the field and out of the courtroom.

Stewardship

Because climbing instructors visit the same crags over and over again, they are in the unique position to see problems as they arise. Whether there are issues with graffiti, trail-braiding, litter, or something else, they are often the first to notice. Noticing is not enough. Climbing instructors should be advocates for the places where they work.

It is not uncommon for instructors to go to work and then go home, leaving the issues surrounding the crag at the crag. Perhaps they clean up some trash while they're in the field, but they don't make much of an effort beyond that. It is essential that instructors work to be more involved in stewardship, local climbing politics, and climbing advocacy.

AMGA Access director Scott Massey removes and replaces an old bolt on Rebel Without a Pause (5.11a) in Red Rock Canyon, Nevada. Prior to working for the AMGA, Scott guided in Red Rock, where he oversaw numerous crag-related stewardship projects.

Many climbing areas have a local climbing stewardship organization. Sometimes these are connected to the Access Fund, and sometimes they're stand-alone organizations. Many advocacy groups focus on a very specific area, like the Friends of Indian Creek, the Las Vegas Climbers Liaison Council, or the Friends of Joshua Tree; whereas others have a much broader scope, like the Washington Climbers Coalition, the Northern Colorado Climbers Coalition, or the Southeastern Climbers Coalition. Regardless of an organization's purview, all of these organizations have one thing in common: They need volunteers.

If you don't have the time to volunteer for an advocacy group, make sure to participate in "Adopt-a-Crag"–style activity days. These usually involve litter cleanup and trail-building activities. They may also include re-bolting projects or the removal of invasive plant species. These events are excellent places to meet other local climbers and to give back to the place that provides you an opportunity to work.

Crag stewardship is not just good for the climber's soul; it's just the right thing to do.

Instructor Meetings

If working with another instructor, plan for informal meetings throughout the instructional day. This allows everyone to stay on the same page. Issues that come up during the day can include anything from safety concerns to instructional problems, from inclement weather strategies to dealing with a difficult student. In other words, these meetings cover the gamut.

If working for an organization or guide service, administrators may have formal meetings or debriefs after each course. If they don't actively provide a debrief session, then take the initiative and offer to meet with them. Most administrators appreciate it when new instructors come to them to talk about their programs.

Finally, if you have the opportunity to meet with the instructional staff on a weekly or monthly basis, take advantage of that. Instructors often work alone or with one or two other people. The more exposure you have to other instructors, their hardships and victories in the field, the better an instructor you will become.

CHAPTER 4

Pedagogy: The Art of Teaching

As climbing instructors, it's easy to get focused on the technical aspects of the job: A cam goes here, a rope goes there, a belay works like this, a lower works like that, etc. When we're with other instructors, we tend to talk about how to run a program at a given crag or how to deal with a certain technical situation. Indeed, our students come to us in part because we're experts in the technical aspects of climbing, but that's not the main reason why they climb with us.

They climb with us because they want to learn.

Musicians, actors, writers, painters, and photographers are artists. They spend years refining every aspect of their craft, becoming better as each day marches by. After decades of criticism and self-assessment, these people become masters.

Pedagogy is the art of teaching. And like the musician or the painter, one must dedicate time and energy to the art in order to become a master.

This chapter provides an introduction to the art of teaching as it pertains to climbing. But this is only an introduction, and it is recommended that aspiring instructors seek out other resources—both master-level instructor mentors as well as written materials on educational theory and technique—to continue moving personal development toward mastery.

Learning Styles

Effective instructors not only demonstrate a wealth of knowledge and expertise, but are also able to convey information about what they know in a way that others can readily comprehend, understand, remember, and then go out and use themselves.

When teaching a figure eight follow-through knot to a group of six novices, something like this typically happens: About half the group gets it right the first time, two people get it right after a few tries, and one person just can't get it right even after multiple tries. Why is this? People have differing learning styles, and it is usually not a question of intelligence, but rather a problem with the way the information is being presented that does not suit their particular learning style. Often, taking a different approach with the presentation of the information will help in comprehension and retention.

The theory of learning styles presented here is based on New Zealand educator Neil Fleming's VAK model. There are a number of different theories out there, but this one is a good introduction to the concept of how people learn.

The three main learning styles are visual, auditory (verbal), and kinesthetic (VAK). And although most people embody some combination of different learning styles, one is usually predominant.

Learning knots at Joshua Tree National Park, California.

Visual learners pick up information most effectively by reading the written word and viewing photos or illustrations. They need to see it to learn it. This group represents the highest percentage of the population (roughly 65 percent), and they learn most effectively from written communication. Visual learners think in pictures and words. They prefer their information presented in a written format as opposed to the spoken word, and usually prefer to take detailed notes when presented with verbal information. They can have difficulty with spoken directions. For example, a verbal description of how to get to some place is likely ineffective to them, but a written description along with a map would prove useful. For this group charts, diagrams, graphs, and visual schematics are highly effective. When teaching a knot to this group, a verbal description is of little help, but presenting the sequence of tying the knot like a schematic diagram, with step 1, step 2, and so forth, may prove more successful.

Auditory, or verbal, learners represent another large segment of the population (around 30 percent) and learn most effectively from the spoken word. They need to hear it to learn it. This group is composed of the most sophisticated speakers, and they relate most effectively to spoken words. They are good listeners and will listen attentively to a verbal presentation and take notes afterward. They benefit from hearing lectures and participating in group discussions. They prefer their information presented in a verbal format, and for them information is not tangible unless it is spoken. They can have difficulty with written directions.

Another, much smaller, percentage of people are kinesthetic learners, who learn by doing, by getting the feel and tactile sensation of performing the steps required to learn a task. They are usually gifted athletes and can learn a knot just by seeing it tied, then tying it once or twice. Kinesthetic learners prefer hands-on learning and can appear slow if information is not presented to them in a style that suits their learning method.

Most people learn most effectively by watching, doing, and reflecting on a particular technique. Around 450 BC the great Chinese philosopher Confucius said: "Tell me and I will forget; show me and I may remember; involve me and I will understand." Various research studies point to the fact that people remember best by watching a demonstration, having a discussion, practicing the skill, then teaching it to others. Military trainers use the EDIP principle (explain, demonstrate, imitate, practice).

When teaching climbing techniques, the climbing instructor should present the topic in a way that most broadly targets all the differing learning styles.

The approach can be simple:

1. Tell (auditory or verbal)
2. Show (visual)
3. Do (kinesthetic)

Using this approach, here is an example of how to teach an abstract concept, such as a complicated knot:

1. Tell. Verbally describe the steps to tie the knot.
2. Show. Demonstrate the knot. Facing in the same direction as the person being taught is helpful.
3. Do. Have the student practice tying the knot.

This is the basic approach, although there are additional teaching methods that will help in memory retention and learning, namely imagery and mnemonic devices. An example of using imagery when teaching the bowline knot: "The snake comes up through the hole, around the tree, and back down through the hole." Attaching a verbal image of an animal or thing is one of the most effective ways to remember an abstract concept.

Mnemonic devices are another form of memory aid. The most common one is the acronym. The military is big on acronyms, like IED (improvised explosive device), SOTG (Special Operations Training Group), etc. In teaching climbing, some common acronyms are ABC (anchor, belayer, climber) or BARCK (buckle, anchor, rope, carabiner, knot).

To most effectively teach climbing techniques, it's best to start with an approach that presents the information for a broad range of learning styles, then try to identify each person's particular learning style in order to aim directly at his or her individual style. If someone is not getting the information, change the approach and present it another way. Use imagery and mnemonics to help students remember key principles (like safety checks or anchoring fundamentals), and chances are they will retain these key concepts throughout their climbing lifetime.

Lesson Planning

Many climbing instructors are natural born teachers. But even the best teachers do a better job when they have a structure to work within. Creating concrete unit and lesson plans provides that structure.

Remember when you were in high school and there was a unit on the Civil War or a unit on *Romeo and Juliet*? And remember when during that unit, you studied the battle of Gettysburg or Shakespearean language? These were individual lessons inside of a larger learning arc, an arc that is referred to as a unit.

In rock climbing instruction a unit could cover something as vast as anchor building, while an individual lesson within that unit might cover something like placing a cam. In other words, a lesson is a bite-size piece of a unit, and a series of lessons together combine to provide the knowledge required to complete a unit.

Student-Learning Objective—This is the overriding goal of the lesson or unit, what students should be able to show after they have received instruction.

Examples of student-learning objectives for units and individual lessons include the following:

Unit Objectives

- Students will demonstrate an ability to pass a climbing gym test.
- Students will demonstrate an ability to build an anchor.
- Students will demonstrate an ability to set up a toprope.

Lesson Objectives

- Students will demonstrate an ability to tie a figure eight follow-through.
- Students will demonstrate an ability to belay effectively.
- Students will demonstrate an ability to use appropriate climbing commands.

Please note that each of the preceding sentences starts with "students will demonstrate an ability to . . ." It's incredibly important for every learning objective to start with this, because it provides a concrete goal that can be measured.

In a lesson plan, start with the student-learning objective, work into the specifics, and then culminate in an evaluation. There are many examples of lesson plans out there, but they all start with a learning objective and finish with an evaluation. Following is a simple outline of a lesson plan and how each part of the lesson functions:

Student-Learning Objective—"Students will demonstrate an ability to . . ."

1. **Set**—Preparation for what the students are about to learn. It could be a complex and creative opening, or a very simple, "this is what you're going to learn today."

2. **Input**—The actual teaching of the lesson.

3. **Guided Practice**—Working with the students until they achieve mastery.

4. **Evaluation**—Evaluating whether the student has learned the requisite material.

Many instructors do a very good job of identifying a learning objective, setting up a lesson, teaching it, and practicing a skill, but often don't evaluate students when they're done. Evaluation is just as important as any other part of the lesson.

Following is a sample plan for a knot-tying lesson:

Student-Learning Objective—Students will demonstrate an ability to tie a figure eight follow-through.

1. **Set**—Explain to students that this is one of the most important knots they will learn. They will need this knot to tie into the rope, and if they want to join a climbing gym, they will be tested on it.

2. **Input**—Demonstrate how to tie the knot. With certain populations you might choose to use a mnemonic (a memory trick) to help the students remember.

Single Pitch Instructor Sample Lesson Plan

Lesson Title: **Timeframe:** Overall timeframe for the lesson:

Student-Learning Objective: Students will demonstrate an ability to . . .

Audience: Brief description of the audience including age, skill level, limitation, etc.

Prerequisites: List any prerequisite training or skills.

Lesson Location and Special Notes: Identify where the lesson will take place. Have a back-up plan in place if the location is being used. Add reminders such as equipment needs, classroom prep, and "don't forget" notes.

Time	Materials
____min	**Set:** Prep the students for what they are going to learn.
____min	**Input:** Provide the content of the lesson.
____min	**Guided Practice:** Work with the students to achieve mastery.
____min	**Evaluation:** Test the students on their mastery of the subject.

Does the lesson reach multiple learning styles?   Yes   No

Instructors new to lesson plans should photocopy this sample plan and fill it out for each lesson they intend to teach.

3. **Guided Practice**—Practice the knot with the students.

4. **Evaluation**—Have all the students show that they know how to tie the knot.

Many less effective climbing instructors don't take the time to build lesson plans. The result is that they learn how to teach through an organic process of trial and error, which is terrible for the students who are forced to work with an instructor on an error day.

A review of the day with input from the students provides valuable feedback from their perspective of how they perceived an instructor's presentation of the topics. This allows the instructor to improve and modify the approach for the next time. Getting feedback from students is key to becoming a better instructor.

The best teachers prepare lesson plans on paper ahead of time and then continue to tweak them over a period of months and years. They use a

structured approach through student feedback and self-assessment and keep track of what works and what doesn't work. They make note of all student-learning objectives and do their best to make sure that their students achieve those objectives.

Master teachers don't just appear out of the woodwork. They work hard every day to be the best.

Learning from Mistakes

Asking a student with some experience to perform a task can tell an instructor a great deal about the student and where to begin. For example, one quick test that can be given to new students is to simply hand them the end of the rope with the instructions: "Go ahead and tie into the rope." The way that they accomplish this easy task tells more about where they're at than even a brief interview.

Another example: When teaching anchoring fundamentals to a group class in a ground-school setting, present a concept with a verbal presentation, a demonstration, and then a hands-on practice (tell-show-do). Give each of the students a scenario (e.g., this is the edge, here are the crack systems you can work with, build your anchor system so that your master point is here, etc.), then let the students build an anchor system to their satisfaction, without constant coaching by the instructor along every step in the process. By letting them finish without instructor input, they are likely to make some mistakes. Then, as a group, go around and critique each anchor system setup. In this way everyone learns from everyone's mistakes. The big plus is that it gives the instructor valuable and instant feedback on whether or not the students have grasped the concepts just presented and shows what they (or we) need to work on to achieve our objective.

This can be a very effective strategy when teaching a lesson to one or two students who have some modicum of anchoring experience but have asked for a refresher course. Start by giving them

Harsh Lessons

In my (BG) career as a rock climbing instructor, I've received training and undergone testing and evaluation of my guiding skills. The toughest lessons, but the most memorable ones, came from the mistakes I made that were critiqued by my mentors and peers. I've also found, in my role as an examiner for the AMGA Single Pitch Instructor exam, that candidates learn more and remember best from their mistakes when it really counts, when they're being scored in a pass or fail test situation. The harshest lessons in life are the ones we don't soon forget.

Anchor rigging session during AMGA Single Pitch Instructor course at Joshua Tree National Park, California.

a specific scenario, like rigging a toprope anchor, and then let them rig it without any coaching. What is seen in the final product of their anchor system helps the instructor decide if he or she needs to start with more basic concepts, or can simply move on and build from a solid foundation to more advanced topics. At this point the instructor can prepare a lesson plan specifically targeted at the students' skill level and build upon their current foundation to reach the objective for the day.

Teachable Moments

A less formal way to present information is to explain and describe the technique as it comes up during the course of the outing or class. These are often referred to as teachable moments. For example, when setting up a climbing situation for students, explain to them as they are tying in to the rope the importance of closing the system by tying a stopper knot in the other end of the rope. If they are on a slab climb and their heels come up, tightening their leg muscles, explaining the correct technique of relaxing the calf muscles and dropping the heels down is a teachable moment. Try to keep it positive. Many teachable moments occur when a simple mistake has been made, and addressing it at that very moment is a great way to teach someone the correct way to do something. The trick is to do it in a positive way that encourages the student to try something new and instantly improve or react positively to a potentially negative situation. Often, the ideal time to address a question is at the moment a particular event that illustrates a key point is occurring. This adds valuable context to the concept.

Taking Kids Climbing

Many kids are natural climbers with an instinctive curiosity and tendency to want to climb things. If you take kids to a rock climbing environment, they'll spontaneously want to explore, climb boulders, and scramble around on the rocks. The obvious danger, however, is that in a fall or slip they can get seriously scraped up, or worse.

Climbing develops muscular strength, balance, and kinesthetic awareness and introduces kids to valuable concepts like problem solving, teamwork, and the success that comes from perseverance and determination.

Toproping is the best method to use to take kids climbing. By the time they are in elementary school, most kids will have reached the level of physical and emotional development to allow them to enjoyably experience climbing in a toprope setting. Nevertheless, there are definitely challenges among this population. It can be difficult to sustain the attention of small children for any sort of sustained lesson. Try to reserve lengthy lessons for those children who seem to show an active interest in acquiring new skills.

It can be very difficult to initiate a lower on a small child. Many of them are so small, the friction of the toprope system is almost as great as the child is heavy. Low-friction belay devices, skinny ropes, and smooth, round-stocked carabiners at the master point can help, but in some cases, the other end of the climbing rope can be used to help retrieve these small climbers.

Selecting climbing equipment for small children can also be challenging. Many small children do not have well-defined hips, so a standard sit harness would be inappropriate for them. There are a number of full body harnesses designed for children, and these should be seriously considered if programming for children becomes frequent. Similarly, small climbing shoes are not always the first thing an instructor considers when selecting shoes for a fleet, but climbing shoes are just as helpful for

How Young Is Too Young?

I (BG) have seen, over the years, cases of precocious children with great balance (as young as age 3) who were physically talented enough to climb and be lowered on a toprope.

a 6-year-old as they are for a 60-year-old. Climbing helmets are also just as important for children as for adults, so having those sizes available will be essential.

Route selection is also a challenge when designing programming for children. Because they are so much shorter than even the shortest adults, they will often use drastically different movement strategies than adults. Smaller holds are more realistic options for smaller hands. Be careful, therefore, of feature-oriented climbs, like face climbs. Sometimes the distances between holds are just unrealistic. Instead, try to find climbs that have a homogenous character for the entire pitch, like crack climbs, chimneys, or slabs. A climb with a uniform character can be climbed by people of all sizes. Set up a short, easy climb on either a low-angle slab or a short wall with abundant hand- and footholds. Teach them the basic climbing signals. For their first time, have them climb up a short distance (say 10 feet above the ground), then go through the signals and have them lean back and weight the rope, get into the lowering position, and get lowered back down to the ground. If a child does not possess the requisite balance to successfully be lowered down the climb, or if they are so small they will require some sort of retrieval system, it is better to know that *before* they reach the top of a climb. Take on a climb in small increments, and don't allow them

AMGA Single Pitch Instructor Tim Page assists as a child lowers. If a child is too light to lower, you may be able to attach the other end of the rope to his harness and pull down to provide more weight.

What Makes a Good Teacher?

Just because you can run 100 meters in 9.7 seconds doesn't necessarily mean you'll be a great track-and-field coach, but it helps. If you have great talent and are able to effectively communicate, you have a winning combination. But I (BG) have seen many world-class climbers who were poor teachers, and many competent but not exceptional climbers who were excellent teachers. What I always look for in my climbing school are instructors who have both traits: talented climbers and patient teachers. Climbers who have mastered all the various climbing techniques at a high level can ultimately be the best teachers, as their mechanics and fundamentals are so sound that they have the innate ability to easily demonstrate key concepts. But they also must be effective communicators and have enthusiasm, patience, empathy, and a desire to share their knowledge in a way that truly benefits their students.

to climb too high above the ground if they're not ready for it. You want the experience to be fun, not terrifying. If they're not yet able to be lowered down, they can swing around on the rope and play on the rock a little bit. There will be a next time. Just familiarizing them with the rope, harness, and equipment can be a good start.

Teaching Climbing Movement

Perhaps the greatest teaching challenge instructors will face involves actually showing people how to use their bodies on the rock, how to actually climb things. The magnitude of the subject is unfathomable. If an instructor looks at a single climb, for example, how many different moves are on that climb? Are there patterns? Are there consistent strategies? The variability of the moves on a single climb is of course compounded by the variety of bodies that will attempt to climb it. This person is tall, this person is short, this person has great upper body strength, this person has none. Even if the bodies were identical, this person is aggressive, that person is contemplative, this person is fearful, that person

climbs with reckless abandon, and so on. Of course, instructors don't get to teach one climb; they are trying to teach dozens of climbs, on dozens of crags, with dozens of rock types, in dozens of climates. It is an immensely dense subject.

This text cannot reasonably cover a topic that large, and it is probably folly for an instructor to attempt to do so as well. Instead, try to focus on what is absolutely essential for a successful experience. When teaching beginners, instructors should first focus on the fundamental difficulties all beginners have: It is difficult to make a bipedal creature move in a quadrupedal manner. Second, teach the specific moves that your students will need to climb in a given area.

Bipeds Becoming Quadrupeds

Most mammals move through terrain on all four limbs, and the coordination of those four limbs does not change when they begin to climb trees, mountainsides, or even rock cliffs. Humans have evolved to move through the world on their hind legs, leaving the forelimbs free to use tools, care for children, etc. It is a strange and counterintuitive proposition to tell a bipedal brain that it must forget its evolutionary programming and move like a quadruped. That is the fundamental difficulty that all beginners have. Even though bipedal locomotion has conditioned them to shift their center of gravity from one foot to the next as they move through terrain, the presence of handholds—the proposition of quadrupedal locomotion—short-circuits their brains. They consistently fail to transfer their center of gravity from one foot to the next when they are holding something in their hands. That is why beginners get pumped when they climb 5.5. They are not necessarily weak, but their upper bodies must exert enormous energy to execute a skill that is normally reserved for their legs.

Unfortunately, knowing and understanding this predicament, even carefully explaining it to a student, doesn't make the learning any less difficult. But, if the predicament is carefully explained to the student, the subsequent coaching will be more precise, more focused on the real problem. Instead of shouting useless and ambiguous feedback to a student, "Trust your feet! Trust your feet! Just stand up!" an instructor can be more precise, "Shift your center of gravity from your low step to your high step!"

Often experienced climbers do not understand how perfectly unconscious their understanding of this fundamental problem is. Their bipedal brains have fully adjusted to quadrupedal locomotion. Climbing instructors need to help their students catch up.

Terrain-Specific Movement

Most likely there will be moves that are specific to the terrain, and instructors should concentrate their coaching on those specific skills. It will be useless to tell students about nuanced and esoteric concepts like flagging or heel hooking if the terrain they are climbing is low angled. There is no need to teach crack climbing if there are no cracks, and so on. Try to find the three or four techniques that are consistent in the course area and teach those skills. On a low-angled climb, for example, students will need to know how to smear. But backstepping and edging are probably extraneous pieces of information. Students will need to focus attention on dynamic weight transfers from a low step to a high step, but they will not need to toe hook or do foot switches. Students will need to mantle, but they will never need to dyno. Be specific; find the movement patterns at the crag and teach those skills.

CHAPTER 5

Baseline Equipment

An office worker can't do anything without a functional computer. A carpenter can't build a house without a hammer. A taxi driver is useless without a working taxi. And a climbing instructor is not a climbing instructor without certain essential tools. An instructor's baseline equipment is composed of the instruments crucial to a successful day of climbing instruction.

Following is a breakdown of the essential baseline equipment required by a professional climbing instructor.

Harness

The modern climbing harness is not only more comfortable than the swami belts of climbing's golden era, but they also are manufactured and sold with incredible variety. A climbing instructor selects two types of harnesses—the instructor harness and the participant harness—from a wide array of options for two essential purposes. In the course of a climbing outing, an instructor will need to use the harness to rack lead protection, carry an array of assistance and anchoring tools, tie into a rope (or two ropes) while also using the belay loop, haul a rope, rappel on one device and transfer to another, and so on. A participant, on the other hand, may never need to carry an extraordinary amount of equipment, may never do any sort of technical multitasking, and may only actually sit in the harness while being lowered. As a result of these two fundamentally different harness applications, a climbing instructor should deploy two different sets of criteria when selecting the best harness for the job. In both cases a harness with a waist belt, leg loops, and a belay loop will be the most comfortable and useful.

When selecting an instructor harness, look for a model that has

- a separate space for belaying/clipping to the harness (belay loop) and tying-in (the hard points of the harness)

Swami Days

I (BG) began climbing before the advent of the modern climbing harness. Instead of a harness, I used a swami belt. I took a 20-foot length of 2-inch-wide nylon webbing (rated at 8,000 lbs.), wrapped it a bunch of times around my waist, and tied it with a water knot. Then I tied my climbing rope around the swami belt with a figure eight follow-through. This setup discouraged **hangdogging** and was rib jarring in a leader fall! Soon we figured out how to add leg loops, which made the rig more comfortable, to say the least!

- gear loops to hold all tools and a rack
- adjustable leg loops (if you'll be climbing in different seasons, with different amounts of clothing)
- comfortable for all-day use

For a participant harness, look for a model that has

- durability to sustain repeated novice use
- simple functionality to expedite instruction and supervision
- adjustability to fit a large of number of body types and sizes

Modern speed buckle.

Modern, lightweight climbing harness.

Top brands include Arc'teryx, Black Diamond, Petzl, Metolius, Trango, Mammut, Misty Mountain, and Camp USA.

Some newer models have webbing with "speed buckles" that are pre-threaded and already doubled back. Other harnesses have the old-school "double pass" buckle, where the webbing belt must be doubled back through the buckle. The instructor should be able to demonstrate how to properly buckle and use each student's harness.

For students, fully adjustable models are convenient and efficient, especially for outfitting groups. Black Diamond, for example, offers a fully adjustable model with speed buckles for sizes extra small through medium, and another model for large to extra large.

Harnesses should be retired when the belay loop becomes frayed or shows signs of wear. For recreational climbers, Petzl recommends using nylon products no longer than seven years, even with minimal use. In an institutional setting, harnesses are retired sooner than that.

Traditional, doubled-back buckle.

Harness with adjustable leg loops.

Helmets

Back in the 1960s and 1970s, very few climbers (probably less than 10 percent) wore helmets. Today it's the opposite. Most climbers wear helmets, particularly in trad climbing areas. The professional standard is for all guides and instructors to wear a helmet and to enforce a helmet policy for their students.

Even in the seemingly benign single pitch environment, rockfall can be a real hazard, especially if there is loose rock at the top of the cliff. Rockfall can occur naturally (from wind or melting snow or ice) but more commonly is caused by other climbers. The most common scenarios are a climber pulling off a handhold or breaking off a foothold while climbing, inadvertently kicking off a rock from the top of the cliff, or causing a rockfall by manipulation of the rope. Be especially aware when other climbers are at the top, rigging anchors and setting ropes, as rocks are easily dislodged by ropes being pulled around. When teaching groups, establish a mandatory helmet zone at the base of the cliff, and then watch for students who are lounging at the base without a helmet.

Students should be taught that while on the cliff or at the top of the cliff, if a rock (or any object) is dislodged, the universal signal is "ROCK!" How loud the signal is yelled can signify the size of the rock. If the warning comes from 100 feet or more away, students can be taught to look up, judge

Helmets help manage risk in the single pitch environment.

the trajectory, and move aside accordingly. If the signal comes from just above, students should be instructed to hunker down and not look up, so as not to get hit in the face. Obviously, wearing a helmet is most important when climbing, belaying from the base of the climb, and hanging out at the bottom of the cliff.

Be particularly alert for rockfall when rappelling, as it can be caused by the rope coming into contact with the cliff, particularly if the climber swings from side to side and especially if there is loose rock on the cliff.

Top brands of climbing helmets include Petzl, Black Diamond, Mammut, and Camp USA.

Ropes

History

Mountaineering's first golden age ended abruptly on July 14, 1865. For Edward Whymper, who led a team of seven climbers up the first ascent of Switzerland's Matterhorn—at the time the last great unclimbed peak in the Alps—both triumph and tragedy were his fate on that great and dreadful summer's day. After reaching the summit the climbers, all tied together with manila ropes, began a tedious descent. One of the party suddenly slipped, pulling several of the others off. While Whymper held fast, clinging to a rock outcrop to avoid being yanked into the abyss, the rope broke, sending four climbers to their death. Later buried in the Zermatt cemetery, the Matterhorn soars above them as their tombstone for all time. Some speculated that the rope had been cut with a knife, but a formal investigation and inspection of the rope revealed the cord had simply parted—broken under the strain.

Through the late nineteenth and early twentieth century, climbing and rappelling ropes were made from natural fibers like hemp, manila, and sisal. While strong enough for many applications, these ropes were ill-suited to the rigors of climbing and rappelling, and subject to mildew and rot.

Nylon, also known by the generic name polyamide, was developed by the Dupont company in 1935. Modern nylon climbing and rappelling ropes that could actually hold up to the forces generated from leader falls were first manufactured in the 1940s, coinciding with the availability of high-quality "nylon 6," allowing the construction of lighter weight ropes that could stretch to absorb great forces and hold more than 2 tons. Nylon is still by far the best material for rock climbing and mountaineering ropes, due to its ability to stretch and absorb the forces created in a fall, making it superior to any other yarns currently available for this application.

Polyester, patented in 1941, has less stretch than nylon and is today widely used in the manufacture of low-stretch ropes used in rescue, fixed lines, rope systems, and rappelling, where dynamic properties are not required.

Early nylon climbing ropes were a three-strand, woven rope with the brand name Goldline. The three-strand twisted construction (called laid construction) consisted of three strands of twisted filaments spiraled into one singular rope. These ropes stretched considerably under body weight, and if you were rappelling or prusiking without contact to the rock, the spiral construction would result in a dizzying spin on your way down.

Kernmantle Ropes

The big step up in rope technology came in 1953 with the advent of the first kernmantle rope, made in Europe. The kernmantle design consists of an outer, tightly woven sheath (mantle) over a core of twisted, parallel fibers (kern). The core of the rope provides most of the rope's strength, and the sheath protects the core from abrasion and damage and reduces friction as the rope runs through carabiners and rappel devices. The kernmantle rope handles better and is more durable than a rope with laid construction.

During the 1950s and into the golden age of big wall climbing in Yosemite during the 1960s,

Deconstructed kernmantle rope showing the braided white interior core under the more tightly woven sheath.

Selection of dynamic ropes from Nomad Ventures climbing shop, Idyllwild, California.

Dynamic Rope Types

Dynamic ropes are sold in single, double, and twin configurations.

A **single rope** (marked on the label with a 1 inside a circle) is the most commonly used rope for rock climbing and rappelling and is used as a single strand.

A **half rope** (marked on the label with a ½ inside a circle) is used primarily for alpine rock climbing and mountaineering and consists of a pair of ropes both tied in to the leader, who alternates clipping one strand at a time into protection. This configuration reduces rope drag through protection and provides two full-length ropes to facilitate a rappel descent.

A **twin rope** (marked with two overlapping circles) is used primarily in alpine climbing and should only be used with the two strands together; each climber ties into both strands and both strands are clipped into points of protection. The big advantage is that it allows for retrievable rappels the length of the rope, and it is lighter than a half rope. A single strand of a twin should never be used alone for any purpose.

Goldline ropes were still the standard, as they were about a third of the price of kernmantle ropes. Once they became more widely manufactured and distributed, with a correspondingly better price, kernmantle ropes became the standard climbing rope worldwide by the late 1960s and early 1970s.

Today the kernmantle rope is the standard design used in climbing, rappelling, caving, canyoneering, vertical rope access, fixed lines, rescue, and life safety ropes. These ropes are made from nylon, polyester, or a combination of these and other synthetic yarns. There are three basic types of kernmantle ropes: dynamic, low-stretch, and static. A dynamic rope is required for situations where a high-impact force can be generated—such as in a leader fall—and therefore is the standard rope for rock climbing, ice climbing, and mountaineering, where the rope will be used for belayed climbing and rappelling. A dynamic rope will typically stretch about 26 to 36 percent during a leader fall (dynamic elongation) and around 7 to 11 percent under body weight (static elongation).

UIAA and CE Certification for Dynamic Ropes

Dynamic ropes sold for rappelling, climbing, and mountaineering are tested and certified to UIAA (Union Internationale des Associations d'Alpinisme) and CE (Conformité Européenne) standards and should bear the UIAA or CE certification on the label. This means that the rope has been tested and certified by a "third party" at one of three UIAA-approved testing facilities to meet the European Norm (EN) 892 and UIAA-101 standard for dynamic rope. To receive this certification, the rope sample must survive at least five UIAA drop tests. This test is done by taking an 80 kg (176 lb.) weight, attaching it to one end of a 9-foot length of rope, then raising it 8½ feet above the anchor and dropping it 15 feet over a 10mm diameter bar (similar to a carabiner) that is anchored approximately 1 foot above where the rope end is anchored. This simulates a fall factor of 1.7 (total distance of the fall divided by the length of rope in the system), which is a very severe fall in climbing situations.

For a single rope, during the first drop, the peak impact force on the rope is measured and must be less than or equal to 12 kN (8 kN for a half rope with a weight of 55 kg) with a corresponding stretch of less than or equal to 40 percent. Twin ropes have the same requirements as a single rope but must survive at least twelve drops without breakage. In addition to the stringent drop test requirements, sheath slippage can be no more than 1 percent, and static elongation under an 80 kg (176 lb.) load can be no more than 10 percent for a single rope and no more than 12 percent for a half or twin rope.

To the best of our knowledge, the only documented rope failures among UIAA-certified ropes were ropes that were cut over sharp edges and one rope with known pre-exposure to sulfuric acid.

Static and Low-Stretch Ropes

For many years the term *static rope* was used to define any low-stretch rope typically used as a rescue rope or as a fixed line for rope access, rappelling, and life safety. As rope manufacturers developed new techniques and technologies to create better low-stretch ropes, the terms *static rope, low-stretch rope, low-elongation rope,* and *semi-static*

Climbing shops sell static and low-stretch ropes from spools, cut to the length you desire.

rope, often used interchangeably, became somewhat ambiguous, especially since all ropes have some stretch, so a more precise definition was needed.

The Cordage Institute, an international rope industry association that disseminates industry standards, defines two categories of non-dynamic ropes: static and low-stretch.

STATIC ROPES

Static is defined as rope with a maximum elongation of less than 6 percent at 10 percent of the rope's minimum breaking strength (MBS). New technology allows manufacturers to create static ropes with virtually no stretch—think of them almost like a wire cable. For example, the Sterling Rope company's ½-inch diameter HTP Static rope stretches only 0.8 percent with a 300-pound load and has a safe working load (SWL) of 908 pounds, which is ⅒ of its MBS of 9,081 pounds.

These ropes should not be used for toprope belaying, but can be used for anchor rigging and fixed lines, although low-stretch is also preferable for those applications since even a slight amount of stretch means a lower impact force on the anchors.

Static ropes generally have poor handling characteristics due to their stiffness and are typically used only for haul lines, high lines, zip lines, and rappelling, where dynamic properties are not required. A static rope should never be used for lead climbing or for belaying, where it may be subject to a high-impact force.

LOW-STRETCH ROPES

The Cordage Institute defines low-stretch as a rope with an elongation between 6 and 10 percent at 10 percent of the rope's MBS. Since a low-stretch rope has relatively little stretch (usually 3 to 4 percent under body weight) compared to a dynamic rope, it is a great choice if you're using it just for toproping and rappelling, but it should not be used for leading. Low-stretch ropes may also be a good choice for rigging anchor extensions and fixed lines because

they are easy to tie knots with, and they reduce potential impact forces when used as a tether or belay.

Dynamic versus Low-Stretch

When buying ropes, the following criteria will help the instructor assess which rope is best for a particular application.

A dynamic rope is required for situations where you'll be using the rope for leading or belaying, where any impact force is anticipated. A low-stretch rope should not be used for lead climbing, because rope stretch is the key to absorbing the energy generated in a leader fall.

For a program involving just toproping, using a low-stretch rope makes a lot of sense, since dynamic rope stretch is often a hazard, or at least a nuisance, in a toprope situation. Picture a 100-foot-high cliff set up as a toprope. At the start of the climb, you'll have 200 feet of rope in the system. Let's say you're belaying a climber using a dynamic rope, with a bit of slack, and the climber falls 15 feet up the route. Let's assume the rope has a static elongation of 9 percent. Do the math: 185 feet times 9 percent equals 16.7 feet. Chances are your climber will find herself on a 16.7-foot bungee cord that eventually returns her to the ground (the thing she is most worried about impacting).

Diameter and Sheath Percentage

Ropes sold for climbing and rappelling commonly range from 9 to 11mm; 10mm is a very popular diameter among climbing instructors, as it's durable yet light and supple. Recently there has been a trend toward ever-thinner ropes. Ropes as thin as 9.4mm in diameter are UIAA rated for lead climbing. But these thinner ropes are generally stretchier and will wear out far more quickly. For toproping, selecting a rope that is thinner than 10mm in diameter often results in having to purchase new ropes more frequently.

Low-Stretch Ropes

I n my (BG) climbing school program, we've used low-stretch ropes for our toproping classes for more than twenty-five years. These low-stretch ropes stretch about 3 to 4 percent under body weight, slightly more in a toprope fall with a bit of slack. From a risk management standpoint, it just makes sense to use a low-stretch rope for toprope situations, especially if you're setting up relatively long routes (up to 100 feet high). I look for a rope with either a CE EN 1891 Type A certification or a National Fire Protection Agency (NFPA) light use certification, with a diameter of between 10 and 10.5mm, to be compatible with various belaying and rappelling devices. I also check the rope's suppleness to ensure the rope will hold knots firmly and handle well. Sterling makes an excellent low-stretch polyamide (nylon) rope called the Safety Pro. I prefer the 10.5mm diameter for good handling and durability for toproping and rappelling.

If using a dynamic rope for toprope belaying, beware of the dangers of rope stretch, and keep the rope taut in situations where the climber is just off the ground or just above a ledge.

Thinner ropes generally stretch more and cut more easily over sharp edges. A thicker diameter rope also affords more friction when used with rappelling devices.

Many manufacturers now provide information on the sheath's percentage of the total weight. A rope with a higher percentage of sheath (40 percent or more) will generally be more durable for rappelling use than one with a lower sheath percentage.

Sharp Edge Resistance

The UIAA has developed a new, optional test for manufacturers to receive a "sharp edge resistant" certification. The test is very similar to the UIAA drop test, although instead of dropping the rope over a rounded bar simulating a carabiner, a sharp edge is used. This is a pass or fail test, and although not a true indicator of durability, it's a good measure of the rope's ability to resist slicing over sharp rock edges. As mentioned earlier, some of the only documented cases of modern climbing ropes breaking in the field have been when the rope was cut over a sharp edge.

Static Elongation

This is a measure of how much the rope stretches under a weight of 80 kg (176 lbs.), telling you how much your rope will stretch during a normal rappel or when someone hangs on the rope. For toproping, rappelling, and fixed rope applications, some instructors prefer a low-stretch rope with a static elongation of around 3 to 4 percent. Most dynamic climbing ropes have a static elongation of about 8 or 9 percent.

Dry or Non-Dry

Nylon, when it gets wet, absorbs water, which weakens the fibers. Nylon ropes can lose much of their strength when wet (at least 30 percent; some studies show over 50 percent loss of strength), so manufacturers sell ropes with a "dry coating" to keep the rope from absorbing water and make it more abrasion resistant. If using a dynamic nylon rope in snow, ice, or wet conditions, a rope with a dry coating is recommended.

Marking the Middle of Your Rope

Many climbers use a black felt tip marking pen to mark the midpoint of their rope. In 2002 the UIAA Safety Commission issued a warning based on testing done by the UIAA and by some rope manufacturers that showed the ink from some marking pens decreased the strength (more specifically, the rope's ability to hold repeated falls in accordance with the EN 892 testing standard) by as much as 50 percent. While this may seem to be a shocking figure, the UIAA president pointed out that "such a marked rope can only break in practice when the 2 or 3 centimeters, which are marked, are placed over a sharp rock edge when the rope is loaded by a fall." While this is a very remote possibility, an instructor should consider other alternatives to identify the midpoint on a rope, or at least use only marking pens sold or recommended by the manufacturer of your rope. Tape is not a good option, as it can slide on the rope or, more likely, become gummy and stick in rappel and belay devices. A good option is to use a "bipattern" rope, which is a rope that changes pattern at the middle without a change in yarns or color. Another option is a "bicolor" rope, which has a color change at the midpoint of the rope. The rope manufacturer changes yarns and joins the yarns together with what is known as an "air splice" (forcing the ends to entwine around each other using extremely high air pressure). The process creates a cosmetic blemish at the yarn change, which the manufacturers say is actually stronger than continuous fibers because of the extra fibers at the splice. Without a middle mark on your rope, to find the middle simply start with both ends and flake the rope out until you reach the middle.

For pure rock climbing in dry conditions, it might not be worth the added cost, as dry ropes are generally more expensive and the coating wears off with repeated toproping.

Rope Length

In the 1970s the standard length for a dynamic climbing rope was 50 meters (165 feet). Today the standard is 60 meters (200 feet), and many climbers use 70-meter ropes (230 feet). These are the standard pre-cut lengths you can buy from a climbing shop. Static and low-stretch ropes are commonly sold in pre-cut lengths and are also sold directly from spools, cut to your desired length. Climbing instructors should select a length that is appropriate for the climbs they intend to instruct, choosing a length that will allow them to work at both the bottom (where the rope will need to be twice as long as the climb is tall) and the top of a given climb. It seems particularly wasteful to carry 70 meters of rope if the average climb in a given area is only 50 feet tall.

Rope Care and Use

Many instructors have access to climbing equipment, including ropes, through pro-purchase programs. Top brands include Sterling, Maxim, Bluewater, Mammut, Edelrid, Edelweiss, Petzl, Millet, and Metolius.

Avoid setting up a climb or rappel where a rope might abrade or cut over an edge. This can severely weaken or ruin your sheath in just one outing! Avoid standing or stepping on the rope, as this can grind sharp pebbles and grit through the sheath and into the core. Minimize the rope's exposure to UV light, as this will weaken the fibers over time. Store ropes in a shaded, dry place.

A dirty rope can be washed in a tub by hand or in a washing machine (preferably a front-loading washing machine, because a top-loading machine's agitator will abrade the rope) with hot water and a soap suitable for nylon. It's not a bad idea to run the machine once with nothing in it before washing the rope to make sure that there is no residual bleach inside. If washing a rope in a bathtub, make sure the tub is free from any chemicals that may damage the rope. It's best to daisy chain the full length of the rope before washing it in a machine to keep it from getting tangled. Let the rope dry by hanging it in a shaded area.

Be vigilant and protect all rope from coming into contact with any chemicals that contain acids, bleaching or oxidizing agents, and alkalines. Acid is the arch enemy of nylon and can severely weaken nylon and polyester fibers. Be extremely cautious to avoid exposing your rope to battery acid or any type of acid that may be encountered in your garage or the trunk of your car. It is wise to store your rope in a rope bag.

It is not a good idea to use a rope without knowing its history. Keep track of its history and age. Most manufacturers recommend keeping a rope for no longer than five to seven years even with minimal use, and no longer than ten years even if the rope has been stored and never used. In an institutional setting, ropes are usually retired well before the manufacturer's recommendation.

Inspect a rope by running your hand over the entire length of the sheath when coiling and uncoiling the rope. Visually inspect for excessively worn areas on the sheath, and feel for irregularities (voids, flat spots, etc.) in the core. The rope should be retired (or cut to a shorter length) if the sheath is excessively worn or frayed, exposing the core, or if there are any anomalies in the core. Multiple fast rappels can burn the sheath of a rope, a result of heat generated by the friction between the rope and rappel device. If the sheath feels glazed or melted, the rope should be retired.

Coiling and Uncoiling Your Rope

With a new rope, take extra care the first time it is uncoiled to prevent kinking. The best method is to simply unroll the rope from the coil, as if pulling it off a spool, holding the rope and rotating the coil until the entire rope is stacked on the ground, keeping the rope free from any twists. Once the rope is in a loose pile, inspect the rope by running it foot by foot through your hands from one end to the other, then coil it with the butterfly coil method.

BACKPACKER OR BUTTERFLY COIL

The backpacker, or butterfly, coiling method puts fewer kinks in your rope. It is also the fastest way to coil a rope, since you start with both ends or from the middle and coil a doubled rope. When coiling from the ends, a good idea is measuring two and a half arm lengths (both arms extended), then begin the butterfly.

MOUNTAINEER'S COIL

Another standard coiling method is called the mountaineer's coil. This is a traditional method that makes for a classic, round coil that can be easily carried over the shoulder or strapped onto the top of a pack.

Knife

Many instructors carry a knife, but it's important to be very careful with when and how it is used. A rope under tension cuts more easily than one not under tension.

Slings and Webbing

In the 1960s and 1970s, 1-inch-wide tubular nylon webbing was the standard sling material, tied into a loop with a water knot or double fisherman's knot. Eventually, sewn slings with bartacked stitching came onto the market and were actually stronger than the same material tied with a knot. Sewn slings are not only stronger but also more secure in that there is no need to worry about the knot loosening and coming untied.

Flat Webbing

Flat webbing is woven solid, as opposed to tubular webbing, which is woven into a hose-like shape. It is stiffer and more abrasion resistant than softer tubular webbing, with a higher tensile breaking strength (Sterling 1-inch flat webbing is rated at 43.5 kN or 9,800 lbs.), which makes it useful for high-strength applications. Its stiffness, however, makes it more difficult to knot and gives it poor handling characteristics, making it unpopular with climbers.

Tubular Webbing

There are two types of tubular nylon webbing: mil-spec and climb-spec.

Since webbing was originally manufactured for military applications, mil-spec means that the webbing meets the standards demanded by the military. Mil-spec has a coarser, rougher-textured weave, with a more pronounced ribbing across the width of the webbing. Climb-spec is a finer, more high-quality weave, without the noticeable ribbing and with a more tightly woven edge. Climb-spec usually tests slightly stronger than mil-spec webbing and is generally more abrasion resistant and more impervious to tearing or slicing over a sharp edge, but both are suitable for climbing applications and both are roughly the same price.

The Bluewater company, known for manufacturing high-quality webbing, says its climb-spec tubular nylon webbing "outperforms normal Mil-spec webbing in strength, flexibility, knotability, and durability. There is minimum exposure to individual fibers as a result of high thread count and fine weave pattern." Bluewater's 1-inch climb-spec

---

What Kind of Knife Is Best?

In thirty years of climbing, I (BG) have never had to cut anything out of a rappel device. I have used a knife to cut off old nylon webbing and cord from rappel anchors, to replace it with new material. In fact, if I'm doing a climb that requires a rappel using a natural anchor such as a tree or block of rock, I'll make sure I have a small knife and extra webbing. I prefer a stainless steel knife with a serrated blade that easily cuts both rope and webbing. Petzl makes several models specifically for climbing, with a folding design that has a round hole on one end to clip into a carabiner. The small and lightweight Trango Pirana has a unique design that can't open up on you when it's folded closed and clipped into a regular-size carabiner.

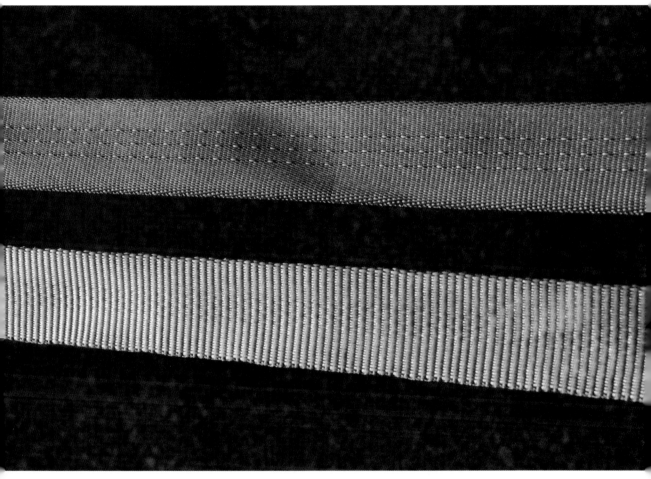

Top: Bluewater 1-inch climb-spec nylon webbing, rated at 18 kN tensile strength (4,047 lbs.).
Bottom: REI 1-inch mil-spec nylon webbing, rated at 17.8 kN tensile strength (4,002 lbs.).

webbing has been tested to over 6,000 pounds loop strength when tied with a water knot.

The Sterling Rope Company's version of climb-spec webbing is called Tech Tape, with a "smoother, denser weave and higher tensile strength" than their mil-spec webbing and a 4,300-pound tensile strength. Sterling's mil-spec webbing is rated to a minimum breaking strength of 4,000 pounds tensile strength and 6,129 pounds in a bartacked sewn loop.

Pre-sewn nylon slings are typically sold in 11/16-inch (18mm) width, bartacked into 24-inch or 48-inch loops with a rating of 22 kN (4,946 lbs.) loop strength.

Climbing shops sell both mil-spec and climb-spec 1-inch tubular nylon webbing from spools, cut to any length desired. Be aware that these spools of webbing contain taped splices where the webbing ends have been joined together with masking tape.

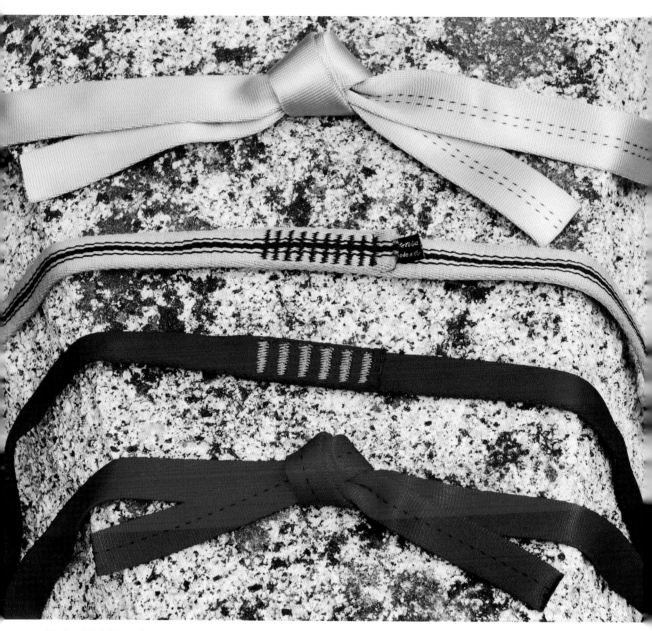

Nylon Webbing Comparison. Top to bottom: 1-inch tubular nylon webbing tied with water knot (Sterling Tech Tape, rated at 4,300 lbs. tensile strength); 18mm Metolius Nylon Sling, rated at 22 kN loop strength (4,946 lbs.); 18mm Black Diamond Runner, rated at 22 kN loop strength; $^{11}/_{16}$-inch Sterling tubular webbing tied with a water knot (rated at 3,000 lbs. tensile strength).

Tape Won't Hold Body Weight

It seems impossible for it to happen, but I (BG) know of two cases where spliced webbing was sold to customers who then used it with only the masking tape joining the webbing together, in one case with devastating results.

One advantage of cut to length nylon webbing is that it can be untied and re-tied around a tree, through a tunnel, or threaded through bolt hangers for a rappel anchor.

The Bluewater company recommends the maximum lifespan of its nylon webbing to be no more than five years, and also recommends retiring a nylon sling if it has been subjected to temperatures above 176 degrees Fahrenheit, is scorched or glazed from a rope being pulled across it, shows signs of UV degradation from being left out in the elements (faded color and/or stiffness), or if it has been exposed to acid or bleach. Like a nylon rope, nylon webbing can lose an appreciable amount of strength when wet or frozen.

Spectra and Dyneema Slings

Spectra slings, introduced in the late 1980s, were lighter, less bulky, and stronger than nylon. Dyneema is a more recent innovation, typically sold in various-length loops sewn with bartacked stitching in 10mm width. Dyneema and Spectra both have almost the identical chemical makeup of high-molecular-weight polyethylene, which, pound for pound, is stronger than wire cable. Most experts say that the manufacturer of Dyneema consistently produces more high-quality fibers than the manufacturer of Spectra material, and most of the climbing and rappelling slings on the market today are made from Dyneema.

Both Spectra and Dyneema slings are constructed from parallel fibers—very strong but with

Tensile Strength vs. Loop Strength

Strength ratings are often given as *tensile strength* and *loop strength*. Tensile strength is tested by a straight pull on a single strand of the material with no knots, done by wrapping the material around a smooth bar (4-inch diameter gives the most accurate test) on both ends and pulling until it breaks. Loop strength is the material tested in a loop configuration, either tied with a knot (in the case of webbing, usually the water knot) or sewn with bartacked stitching. In general, webbing loop strength when tied with a water knot is about 80 percent of twice the tensile breaking strength, and bartacked sewn webbing loop strength is generally about 15 percent stronger than the same material tied with a water knot, depending upon the quality and number of bartacks.

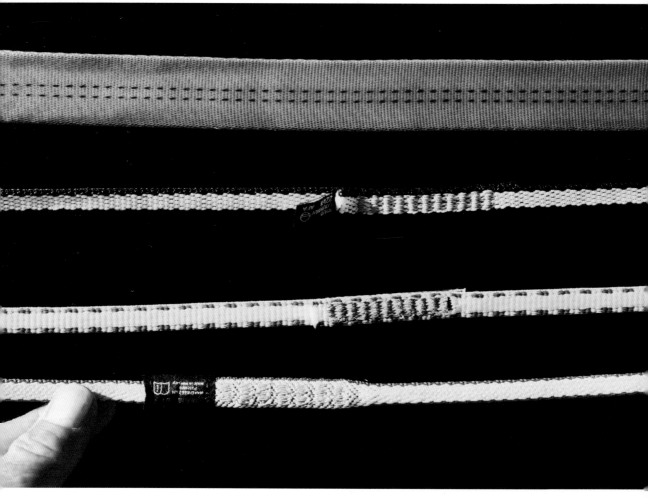

Dyneema Sling Comparison. Top to bottom: 1-inch tubular nylon webbing (for comparison); Wild Country 10mm Dyneema sling (22 kN or 4,946 lbs.); Black Diamond 10mm Dynex Runner (22 kN); Mammut 8mm Dyneema Contact Sling (22 kN).

high lubricity, which means the material itself is inherently slick. That is the reason it can only be purchased in sewn loops—it does not hold knots well. *Do not cut a Spectra or Dyneema sling and re-tie it with a water knot!*

Both Spectra and Dyneema have a lower melting point than nylon (around 300 degrees Fahrenheit for

Dyneema/Spectra compared to nylon's melting point of around 480 degrees). The lower melting point, along with the inherent slipperiness, make Spectra and Dyneema slings a poor choice for tying friction hitches like the prusik, klemheist, or autoblock, compared to 5mm or 6mm diameter nylon cord.

In a pinch, if required to use a sling to tie a

Girth-hitching two Dyneema slings together can decrease their strength by 50 percent, but for most climbing situations, this is not a concern since the loop strength is 5,000 pounds to begin with.

Both Spectra and Dyneema fibers do not retain dye and cannot be colored, so the fiber is distinctive in that it is always white. Manufacturers add a blend of nylon to Spectra and Dyneema, usually in a distinctive border pattern, and it is likely that in the future there will be more nylon in the mix. The Metolius company recently came out with 13mm width slings that are a blend of 36 percent Dyneema and 64 percent nylon.

When using Spectra or Dyneema slings, think of them like a wire cable—they have no stretch, even with nylon blended into the weave. Avoid tying knots with them—it can be almost impossible to untie a simple overhand knot in the newer, thinner Dyneema after it has been seriously weighted. Wild Country warns that the material loses a hefty percentage of its strength (around 50 percent) when tied in a simple overhand knot or girth-hitch—a property that nylon does not possess. The best way to use a Spectra or Dyneema sling is clipped to carabiners. If using them in a sling-to-sling configuration, either basket one sling over another, or use a properly tied girth-hitch.

When buying slings for rappelling, 1-inch or $^{11}/_{16}$-inch width tubular nylon webbing will be the most versatile material for rigging rappel anchors, as it can be cut to a desired length and tied with a water knot. Double-length (48-inch) sewn nylon slings are also handy for tethering into anchors and extending a rappel device away from the harness. The UIAA states that sewn slings should have a minimum load-bearing capacity of 18kN.

Recent studies show that dirty slings are weaker than clean ones. The Mammut company suggests that "to maintain the quality and safety of your slings, you need to clean them regularly." Mammut recommends to "clean soiled slings in hand-hot water with a small amount of mild detergent or in a delicates machine cycle up to 30 degrees centigrade (86 degrees Fahrenheit). Rinse in clear water. Leave to dry in shade."

friction hitch, use a nylon one over a Dyneema or Spectra sling, as nylon will grip better. The newer, thinner (10mm width) Dyneema slings will work for friction hitches, and they do possess some nylon in their construction, but if they start to slide on a rope when under load, the friction will generate heat, which could potentially weaken the sling.

Cords and Cordelettes

A good all-purpose cordelette is 7mm diameter nylon cord, about an 18- to 20-foot length tied into a giant loop with a double fisherman's knot or a double overhand flat bend.

Cordelettes made with a Spectra or Dyneema core and nylon sheath have incredibly high strength and low stretch. Pound for pound, Spectra and Dyneema are stronger than steel (and is the material used in body armor for the military), but both Spectra and Dyneema lose an appreciable amount of strength when tied with knots. Because these cords are so light and strong, with less bulk to carry, they have become popular, especially for rock climbing. The Bluewater company markets the 5.5mm diameter Titan Cord, with a Dyneema core and nylon sheath, rated at 13.7 kN (3,080 lbs.). They say its "combination of high strength, low elongation and light weight provides superior characteristics over other combinations. Dyneema does not lose significant strength with repetitive flexing and offers a huge increase in abrasion and cut resistance over other materials. Bluewater Titan Cord can be cut and sealed with a hot knife. We recommend a triple fisherman's knot for tying 5.5 Titan into loops."

Ideal Cordelette

I (BG) prefer a length that allows me to double the cordelette within the span of my outstretched arms. My favorite brand is Sterling, whose 7mm diameter nylon cord is rated at 12.4 kN (2,788 lbs.) and tests over 5,000 pounds when tied into a loop with a double fisherman's knot.

In recent years high-tech cords utilizing aramid fibers (namely Technora) for the core, with a nylon sheath, have become popular. Aramid fiber has extraordinary tensile strength (stronger than Spectra or Dyneema) with low stretch and an extremely high melting point (900 degrees Fahrenheit), making it difficult to cut and melt. The best way to cut it is with wire cable cutters. Then milk the nylon sheath over the end and seal it by melting the nylon with a lighter. The Sterling 6mm Powercord has a Technora core and nylon sheath, with a single strand breaking strength of around 19 kN (4,271 lbs.); and the 5mm Tech Cord, sold by Maxim/New England Ropes, with a 100 percent Technora core and polyester sheath, rates at a whopping 5,000 pounds tensile strength.

However, at the 2000 International Technical Rescue Symposium, Tom Moyer presented a paper titled "Comparative Testing of High Strength Cord" that revealed some startling deficiencies in Technora and other high-tech cords. Testing showed that with repeated flexing, aramid fibers break down much more quickly (losing strength) than good old-fashioned nylon. In his study a flex cycle test was performed on various cordelettes. The cord sample was passed through a hole in a steel fixture, flexed 90 degrees over an edge, and loaded with a 40-pound weight. The steel fixture was rotated back and forth 180 degrees for 1,000 bending cycles, then the cord's tensile strength was tested (single strand pull test) at the section that had been flexed. The Technora sample showed a remarkable loss of nearly 60 percent of its strength, while Sterling 7mm nylon cord and 1-inch tubular nylon webbing showed no strength loss at all. Bluewater Titan Cord (Spectra core/nylon sheath) showed a few hundred pounds of strength loss, but was nowhere near the drastic loss of Technora. Further research is warranted. The big advantage of these high-tech cords is their low weight, high strength, and low bulk, which is advantageous for situations like multi-pitch rock climbing and canyoneering.

Cord Comparison. Top to bottom: Bluewater 5mm Titan Cord tied with triple fisherman's knot (Dyneema core/nylon sheath, tensile strength 13.7 kN or 3,080 lbs.); Sterling 6mm Powercord tied with triple fisherman's knot (Technora core/nylon sheath, tensile strength 19 kN or 4,271 lbs.); Sterling 7mm Nylon Cordelette tied with double fisherman's knot (nylon core/nylon sheath, tensile strength 12.4 kN or 2,788 lbs.).

If using these high-tech cords, be sure to tie the cordelette with a triple fisherman's knot, and consider replacing them more often with high use. Keep in mind that the price tag on the high-tech cords is roughly twice as much as nylon. The bottom line is this: For an all-purpose cordelette, it is hard to beat old-school nylon—a 7mm diameter nylon cord is a good choice because it is thick enough to be used in a single loop application, like a personal tether. Narrower 5mm and 6mm cord are great to tie friction hitches like the prusik, klemheist, and autoblock, but these smaller-diameter nylon cords don't provide enough tensile strength to be used as a critical link. When buying this accessory cord to be used primarily for friction hitches, buy the softest, most pliable cord that you can find; a stiff cord won't grip as well. Also, be aware of the difference between 5mm nylon accessory cord (typically rated at 5.2 kN or 1,169 lbs.) and 5mm high-tenacity cord (like Bluewater Titan Cord rated at 13.7 kN (3,080 lbs.) As mentioned, 5mm nylon is less useful as a cordelette, while a 5mm high-tenacity cord offers a much greater tensile strength for anchor building and critical link applications.

Carabiners

Carabiners are used primarily to attach various links (like slings and rope) together in the anchor or belay chain. Locking carabiners are used in critical applications and in conjunction with belay and rappel devices. Carabiners come in a variety of shapes: oval, D-shaped, and pear-shaped.

The basic design is of aluminum alloy, with a spring-loaded gate on one side. The spine of the carabiner is the solid bar stock opposite the gate. The small protrusion on one end of the gate is called the nose, and this will tell you which way

Carabiners come in a dazzling array of designs for various applications. Top row (left to right): asymmetrical D, regular D, oval, wiregate D, bentgate D. Bottom: pear-shaped locking. The most useful carabiners for toproping are ovals, Ds, and pear-shaped locking. Bentgate carabiners are used primarily for sport climbing (on the rope-clipping end of a quickdraw).

the gate opens by visual observation. The basic design has a small pin on the gate that latches into a groove on the nose end. The preferable "keylock" design eliminates the pin, and the gate and bar come together in a machined notch. A wiregate carabiner has a wire under tension serving as the gate, providing a wide opening because of its slim mass and eliminating "gate flutter," which is a vibration of a normal solid gate during a fall or peak loading of the carabiner.

Oval carabiners are useful for racking gear, and for use in sets of two or three for connecting the climbing rope to the toprope anchor master point. Because of their symmetry, the gates can be opposed and reversed, and the carabiner configuration retains its oval shape. Two opposed and reversed ovals can also be used in lieu of one locking carabiner at any critical junction in the anchor system, in situations where there are no additional locking carabiners and extra security at a key point is needed. Three opposite and reversed ovals are the equivalent of two opposite and reversed locking carabiners.

Locking carabiners are used for critical links and applications where it is absolutely imperative that

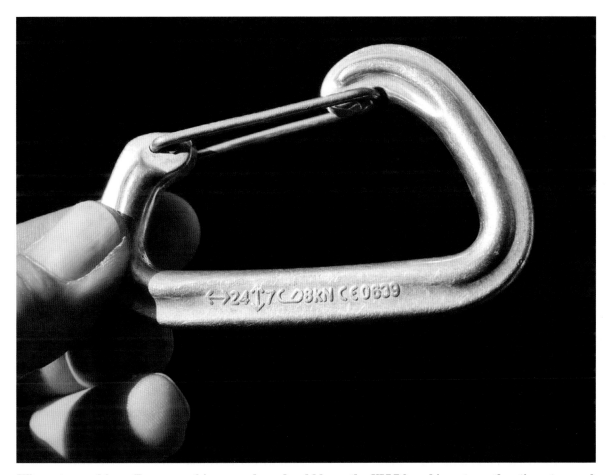

Wiregate carabiner. Every carabiner you buy should have the UIAA breaking strength rating stamped on the spine.

Two oval carabiners with the gates properly opposed and reversed.

Three ovals opposed and reversed at a toprope anchor master point.

the carabiner gate stays closed, like on a rappel or belay device, at a critical link in the anchor system, or when attaching the belayer's climbing rope to the anchor.

D-shaped carabiners have the strongest configuration, since when the carabiner is loaded on the major (long) axis the weight naturally is loaded closest to the spine. For this reason a locking D is a good choice for a belay/rappel carabiner. A locking pear-shaped carabiner is useful for many applications because of its wide aperture on one side. It's a good carabiner to use with a Munter hitch, and a great carabiner to pair up for use at the toprope

anchor master point. When using two opposed and reversed pear-shaped locking carabiners, the symmetry is maintained (unlike an asymmetrical D shape), and the climbing rope runs smoothly through the carabiners.

The most common locking carabiner is the screwgate. The screwgate locking carabiner is just that, a mechanism with a collar that screws shut over the nose of the carabiner. Obviously, with a screwgate locking carabiner, it is important to remember to lock it, and it's an essential habit to always check locking carabiners to make sure they are locked. Check them with a close visual

Two pear-shaped locking carabiners with the gates opposed and reversed on a toprope anchor master point.

Locking carabiners (left to right): Petzl William Triac, Petzl William Ball Lock, Black Diamond Twistlock, Black Diamond Screwgate.

inspection, and also by pressing on the gate (squeeze test) for an additional precaution.

If you're absentminded, or occasionally find yourself not locking a screwgate carabiner, consider buying an autolock or twistlock carabiner. The twistlock design has a spring-loaded gate that locks automatically, and there are several autolocking designs on the market that have a tri-action mechanism that must be manipulated (like pushing the gate upward, then twisting the gate to lock it; or pressing a button, then twisting open the gate), but some climbers find these difficult to use. Interestingly, for industrial workers in the Industrial Rope Access environment (rappelling and rope ascending on the faces of dams, buildings, and bridges), OSHA standards require autolocking carabiners, as does the tree-trimming industry.

The UIAA has determined the following strength ratings for a carabiner to be CE certified.

For oval carabiners:

- Closed gate strength, major (long) axis: 18kN (4,047 lbs.)
- Minor axis (cross-loading) strength, closed gate: 7kN (1,574 lbs.)
- Major axis strength, gate open: 5kN (1,124 lbs.)

For regular D-shaped carabiners:

- Closed gate strength, major (long) axis: 20 kN (4,496 lbs.)

- Minor axis (cross-loading) strength, closed gate: 7kN (1,574 lbs.)
- Major axis strength, gate open: 7kN (1,574 lbs.)

For locking carabiners:

- Closed gate strength, major (long) axis: 20 kN (4,496 lbs.)
- Minor axis (cross-loading) strength, closed gate: 7kN (1,574 lbs.)
- Major axis strength, gate open: 6kN (1,349 lbs.)

An important thing to remember with carabiners is that a carabiner is only about one-third as strong if it's loaded with the gate open. For this reason, keep a few things in mind when using a carabiner:

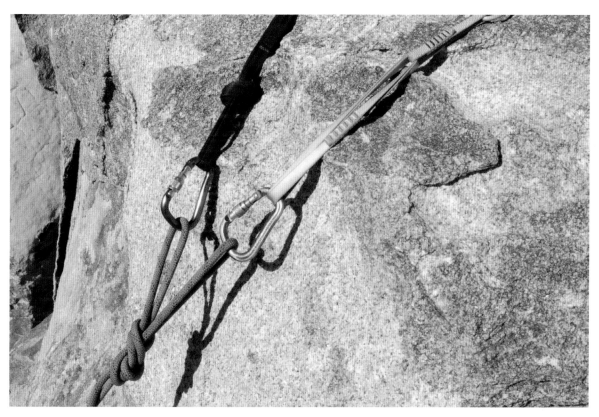

Carabiners should always be loaded on the major axis.

Bad. Never load a carabiner in three directions as shown here.

Very bad. Never load a carabiner on the minor axis or with a force outward on the gate.

- Always load the carabiner in the proper direction—on the major, or long, axis.
- Do not cross-load a carabiner (on the minor axis) or load it in three directions (called triaxial loading).

- Do not load a carabiner over an edge of rock—this can open the gate when the carabiner is loaded, and two-thirds of the carabiner's strength will be lost.

Ovals

I (BG) have used three ovals for thousands of client days without incident. Simply oppose and reverse the outside carabiners to the middle one. The wide radius created by the three carabiners provides a stable platform for the rope and tends not to flip sideways as often as two locking, which can pin the rope against the rock while lowering if the climber's (weighted) strand is on the outside, away from the rock.

Three steel ovals with the gates opposed and reversed at a toprope anchor.

What's in the Pack?

I (BG) prefer a pack that has accessory straps and buckles so I can strap a rope on the outside of the pack. In addition to my rack, slings, cordelettes, belay devices, helmet, shoes, harness, food, water, headlamp, knife, and extra clothing, I carry two first-aid kits. One is a small "patch kit" with small bandages, tape, and a blister kit for minor cuts, scrapes, and blisters. Inside this one I'll also have NSAIDs (aspirin and ibuprofen), acetaminophen, and Benadryl. I also carry a roll of athletic tape. For client care I carry extra sunscreen, lip balm, a trash bag, and a squirrel-proof container for food storage.

My larger first-aid kit is a trauma kit complete with trauma shears, heavy absorbent pads, tape, large bandages, roller gauze, a pocket mask, a couple of Sam splints, and two epi pens.

An instructor's kit should include a communication device (e.g., cell phone, satellite phone, or walkie-talkie), pen and paper (SOAP notes if you're a WFR), and a written emergency response plan with standard operating procedures and appropriate actions for specific scenarios.

Retire a carabiner if it shows a groove from excessive rope wear, or if the gate is no longer in alignment with the body of the carabiner after it has been dropped a considerable distance. If the gate is sticky, washing it with soap and water and using some graphite lubricant will usually take care of the problem.

In the professional realm, the industry standard for attaching the climbing rope to the toprope anchor master point is either two locking carabiners or three oval carabiners with the gates opposed and reversed.

When doing a lot of toproping, aluminum carabiners actually wear rather quickly, developing noticeable grooves. When this happens, they should be retired. Petzl recommends retiring a carabiner with 1mm of wear, about the thickness of a dime. Also, worn-off aluminum particles get on the rope and on the belayer's hands. Using steel ovals solves this problem, as steel is far more durable and wears much more slowly than aluminum.

The Instructor's Pack

A climbing instructor is constantly striving to select the perfect tool for a given task. The instructor's pack is no exception. It should be large enough to hold everything an instructor will need to run an outing and be prepared for emergencies. For most, the best pack is large, about 4,000 to 5,000 cubic inches, and any items that do not fit inside the pack (like a rope or a helmet) are strapped down firmly. A climbing instructor should be able to move through terrain with grace and balance, without swinging or dangling encumbrances, prepared to deal with all contingencies.

CHAPTER 6

Knots and Hitches

What knot should I use here? What hitch should I use there? The answer isn't always obvious. Many knots and hitches accomplish the same thing and work equally well in similar applications. Others do not.

An instructor's job is first to determine which knot or hitch is appropriate for the technical task at hand and, second, to develop strategies for teaching knots and hitches appropriate to a given lesson.

The following pages discuss a wide array of baseline knots and hitches used regularly by Single Pitch Instructors. Certainly there are many more that could be acceptably used in a single pitch setting or taught to students with specific learning objectives, but these represent a fundamental standard of knowledge that every instructor should hold.

Loop Knots

Loop knots are tied by taking two strands of rope (called a bight) and wrapping them back over themselves so that the knot does not slide, or by taking the end of the rope and tying it back over the standing part so the knot does not slide. Loop knots are used to clip the rope into a carabiner, or to tie around an object.

Overhand Loop

This is the simplest knot used to form a loop. It requires less rope to tie than the figure eight. For most applications, however, the figure eight loop is preferable because it tests slightly stronger than the overhand loop and is easier to untie in small-diameter cord.

Knot Terminology

Bend: Two ropes tied together by their ends.

Bight: Two strands of rope where the rope is doubled back on itself.

Load strand: The strand of the rope that bears all the weight.

Hitch: A knot that is tied around another object (such as a carabiner or rope).

Standing end: The part of the rope that the end of the rope crosses to form a knot.

Tag end: The very end of a rope, or the tail end that protrudes from a knot.

Overhand loop.

Finished overhand loop.

Figure Eight Follow-Through

This is the standard knot that climbers use for tying the rope to their harness. It can also be used to tie a rope around an object like a tree or through a tunnel. Climbers have gravitated toward this knot over the years because it is strong, secure, and easy to recognize when tied correctly. Instructors like it because it is easy to teach, and the uniform nature of the knot enables quick inspection and supervision. When tied correctly, the knot is tight, with a 5- to 8-inch tail, and it has bilateral symmetry because the initial figure eight and its follow-through strand are always parallel.

A well-dressed figure eight follow-through has bilateral symmetry. The original strand of rope from the initial figure eight and the follow-through strand are parallel through each curve of the knot. As a result, if a viewer were to draw an imaginary line through the middle of the knot, vertically or horizontally, the halves of the knot would reflect each other in shape, size, and general appearance. This bilateral symmetry gives the knot its signature uniformity, making it easy to recognize from a distance.

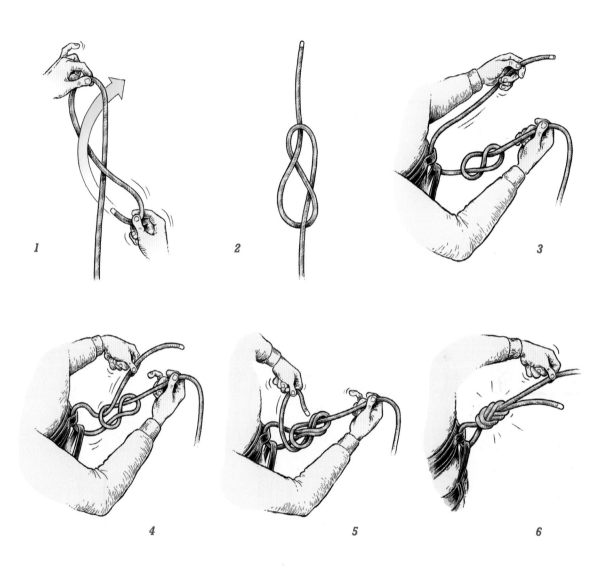

1

2

3

4

5

6

Check the harness manufacturer's guidelines for information on how to properly tie the rope to the harness. For harnesses with belay loops, generally follow the same path as the belay loop, which goes through two tie-in points on the harness. Tie the figure eight so that its loop is about the same diameter as your belay loop. The figure eight knot does not require a backup knot.

Figure Eight Loop

Another standard climbing knot, the figure eight loop is used for tying off the end of a rope, or for tying a loop in the middle, or "bight," of a rope. It is also commonly referred to as a "figure eight on a bight."

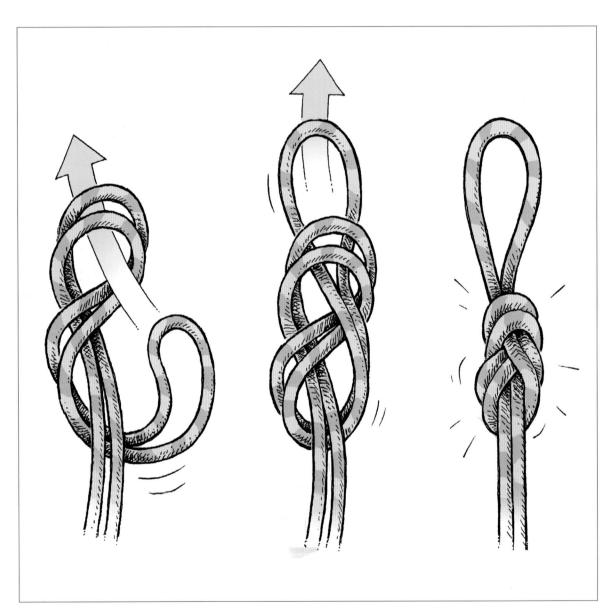

How to tie a figure eight loop.

*Finished figure eight loop
clipped to an anchor.*

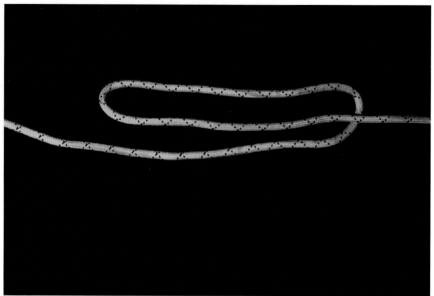

In-line Figure Eight

Also known as a directional figure eight, this knot, like the clove hitch, can be used to tie off a series of anchors in a line. It takes some practice to master this knot, but some find it easier to use than a clove hitch.

Cross the strands to form a simple loop.

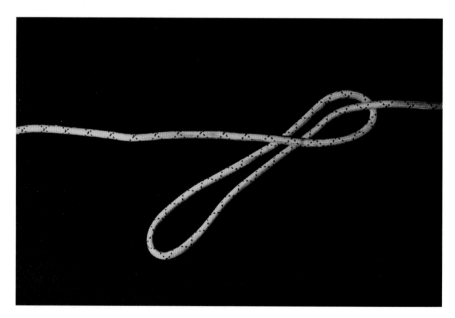

Cross a bight under the single strand.

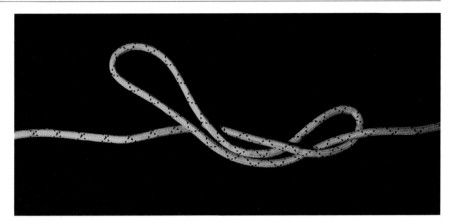

Cross the bight over the strand.

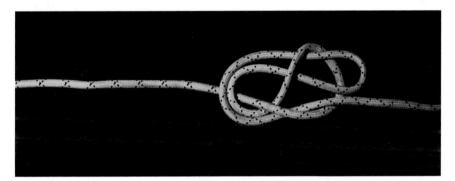

Thread the bight back through the loop you've just formed.

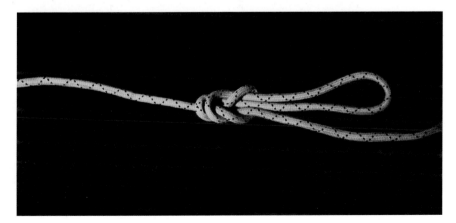

Finished in-line figure eight.

Bowline

Boy Scouts were taught this knot with the saying "the rabbit comes up through the hole, around the tree, and back down through the hole." The bowline is very useful to tie the rope around something, like a tree, block of rock, or tunnel in the rock. It is important to note that a bowline knot requires a backup, as weighting and unweighting the knot easily loosens it. Always tie half of a double fisherman's knot to back it up. One advantage of the bowline is this same feature—it is very easy to untie after it has been weighted, so it is used regularly by professional riggers.

Tying the Bowline

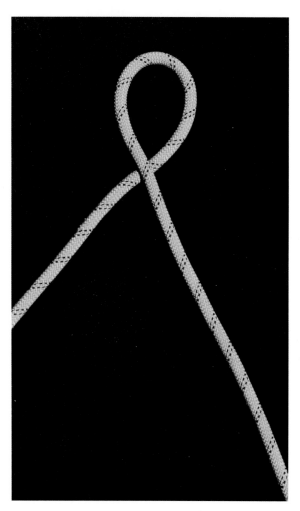 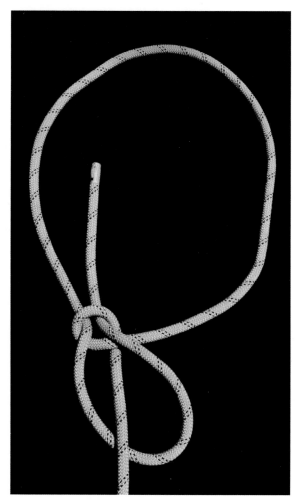

Tying the bowline. The bowline should always be tied with a backup, shown here with half a double fisherman's for the backup knot (final photo).

Double Loop Knots

BHK

The BHK, an acronym for "big honking knot," is technically a double overhand on a bight, used to create a redundant master point. It is commonly used for toprope anchor extensions and master points using rope.

Tying the BHK ("Big Honking Knot")

1 Start by taking a doubled bight about 4 feet long.

2 & 3 Then tie an overhand loop on all four strands.

Master point toprope extension using a BHK and three steel oval carabiners with the gates opposed and reversed.

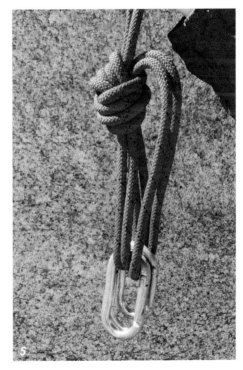

4 & 5 For greater security, take the single loop and hitch it all the way back around the body of the two-loop knot or clip it into the carabiners on the master point.

Double Loop Figure Eight

This knot is used primarily to clip in to or equalize two anchor points. If the two loops are used together at a master point, however, they are not redundant, due to the configuration of the knot.

Tying the Double Loop Figure Eight

Take a bight of rope and cross it back over itself, forming a loop.

Take two strands of the bight and wrap them around the standing part, then poke them through the loop.

To finish, take the loop at the very end of the bight and fold it down and around the entire knot you've just formed.

The double loop figure eight is a great knot to use to equalize two gear placements. You can manipulate the knot by loosening one strand and feeding it through the body of the knot, shortening one loop, which makes the other loop larger.

Double Loop Bowline

This knot is handy for equalizing two anchor points or clipping in to a two-point anchor. It can shift when weighted, so always back it up with a half a double fisherman's if the tail end is near the body of the knot.

Tying the Double Loop Bowline

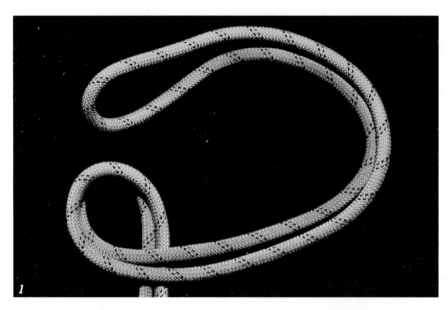

Take a bight of rope and cross it over the standing part.

Thread the bight through the loop you've just formed.

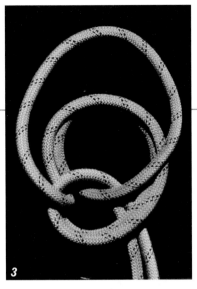

Configure the end of the bight in a loop above the rest of the knot.

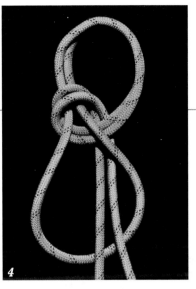

Flip the loop down like a hinge behind the rest of the knot.

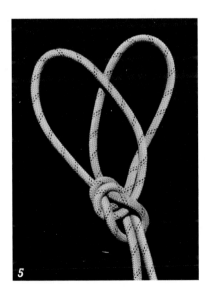

Pull on the two loops until the end of the bight tightens at the base of the knot.

The two loops can be adjusted by feeding one strand into the body of the knot, which alternately shortens one loop and lengthens the other.

Knots for Webbing

Nylon webbing is a slick material that should be tied with caution: There have been many accidents where poorly tied knots in nylon webbing have failed. The two recommended knots for tying nylon webbing into a loop are the water knot (also known as the ring bend) and the double fisherman's knot (also known as the grapevine knot). When tying the water knot, your finished tails should be a minimum of 3 inches in length. It is important you tighten the water knot properly, as it has a tendency to loosen if tied slackly in a sling that is being used over time.

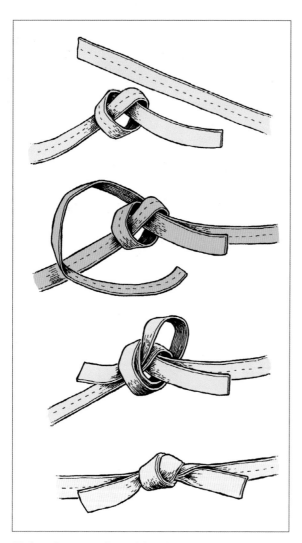

Tying the water knot (ring bend).

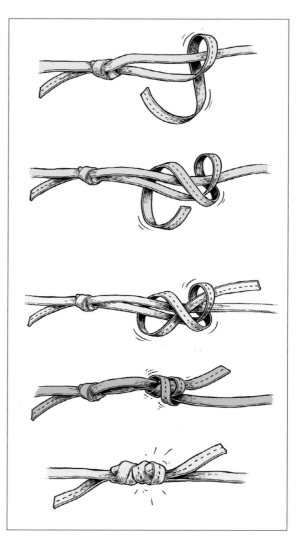

Tying nylon webbing with a double fisherman's (grapevine) knot.

The water knot.

Why would you ever use nylon webbing tied with a knot as opposed to a sewn runner? A sewn nylon runner is stronger than the same material tied with a knot. The answer is for rappel anchors when the slings are tied around a tree or through bolt hangers. It is also sometimes useful to untie the knot, thread it through something (like a tunnel), and re-tie it.

The double fisherman's knot is also a good knot to use to tie nylon webbing into a loop, although it does require more length of material to tie and is very difficult to untie after it has been seriously weighted.

Bends

A bend is a knot that joins two ropes or lengths of cord together. These knots are used to tie your cordelette into a loop, and also to tie two ropes together for rappelling.

Figure Eight Bend (aka Flemish Bend)

A variation of the figure eight follow-through, this knot can be used to tie two ropes together. It has superior strength and is easy to untie after it has been weighted. It is simply a retraced figure eight. On 9mm to 11mm diameter rope, tie it with the tails a minimum of 5 inches long.

The figure eight bend.

Double Fisherman's Knot

This is the preferred knot to use for joining nylon cord into a loop to make a cordelette or prusik loop. It is also a very secure knot to tie two ropes together for a double-rope rappel, but can be difficult to untie.

Tying the double fisherman's knot (aka grapevine knot). When tying 7mm nylon cord, leave the tails about 3 inches long.

Triple Fisherman's Knot

For 5mm and 6mm diameter high-tech cord (i.e., Spectra, Dyneema, Technora), a triple fisherman's knot tests slightly stronger than the double fisherman's. (Moyer, Tom, Paul Tusting, and Chris Harmston [2000]. http://user:xmission.com/~tmoyer/testing/High_Strength_Cord.pdf. 2000 International Technical Rescue Symposium.)

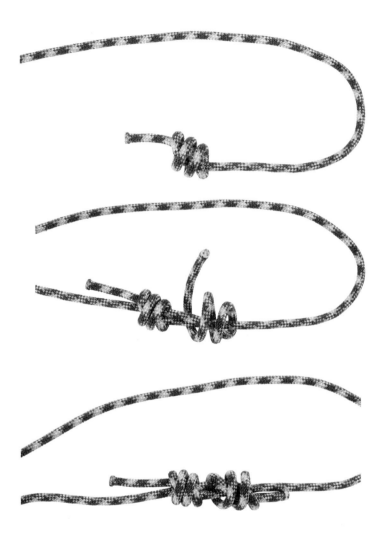

To tie a triple fisherman's, make three wraps before feeding the cord back through.

The triple fisherman's knot.

Knots for Joining Two Ropes

Standard knots for joining two ropes include the double fisherman's knot and the figure eight bend. The double fisherman's is more difficult to untie than the figure eight bend once weighted; the figure eight bend, while relatively easy to untie, is bulky. Tie these knots with a minimum of 3 inches of tail, and carefully tighten the knots before using them. A stiff rope makes it harder to cinch the knots tight, so be especially careful with a stiffer rope.

Which knot to use should be based on several variables. If the ropes differ drastically in diameter, or are very stiff, the most foolproof knot is the figure eight bend, backed up with half a double fisherman's on each side. This is a bulky knot, but it provides a real sense of security.

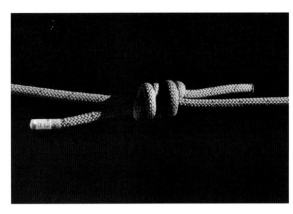

Double fisherman's knot.

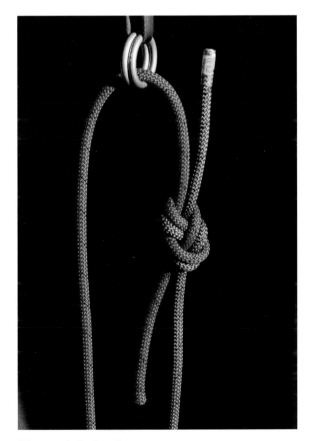

Figure eight bend.

Figure eight bend with fisherman's backups.

Flat Overhand (aka Euro Death Knot)

How this knot received the "Euro Death Knot" moniker is unclear. Most likely the knot was initially adopted by Europeans and deemed unsafe when first seen by American climbers unfamiliar with its use. In reality, it is rarely responsible for incident or injury. In one such rappelling accident in recent times (in the Tetons, September 1997), the flat overhand failed when it was sloppily tied with too short of a tail. Ironically, former *Rock and Ice Magazine* editor George Bracksieck wrote in July of that year that "the one-sided overhand knot (tails parallel and together) remains the best knot for rappelling. . . . Be sure to leave plenty of tail and to set it snugly." After analyzing the accident, Grand Teton ranger Mark Magnusun wrote: "I intend to do some additional research in an effort to gain information on the overhand knot used for joining ropes, the origin of the 'Euro-death' nickname, and incidents of other failures."

Flat overhand knot.

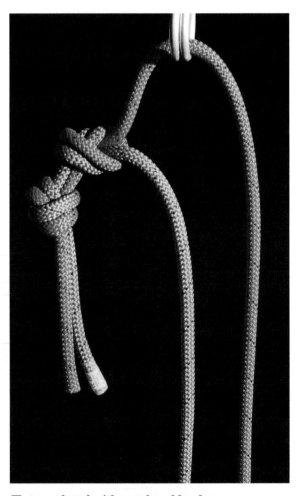

Flat overhand with overhand backup.

From 1999 to 2009 various tests revealed the flat overhand to be roughly 30 percent weaker than the double fisherman's for tying two ropes together, but still plenty strong for rappelling situations. Testing also revealed that it was virtually impossible to get the knot to fail, as long as it was tied with a suitable-length tail and properly tightened.

Petzl, a leading manufacturer of rappelling devices, recommends the flat overhand as the knot to use for joining two rappel ropes together, as long as the ropes are of similar diameter and the tail is a minimum of 20 centimeters (8 inches).

The flat overhand has become widely adopted as the knot for joining two rappel ropes of similar diameters because it is easy to tie and easy to untie after it has been weighted, and it presents a clean profile when pulled down the cliff as the ropes are retrieved, thus less likely to jam in a crack. For added security it can be easily backed up simply by tying another flat overhand above the first one, although this adds bulk.

That being said, there are a few cautions: It is not recommended for tying together two ropes of drastically differing diameters (e.g., 7mm to 11mm), or for use on very stiff ropes. The bottom line is that the knot should be used with discretion, well tightened (pull hard on all four strands), and tied with a long tail (minimum of 8 inches).

The flat overhand is a poor choice for use with nylon webbing, and it has been responsible for rappel anchor failures where it was tied in webbing with a very short tail. The flat eight is even more dangerous if tied with short tails, especially in nylon webbing, and has been responsible for numerous accidents, as it inverts at shockingly low loads when the knot rolls inward and collapses.

Hitches

A hitch is a knot that is tied around something. A friction hitch is a knot tied with a cord or sling around another rope, utilizing friction to make the knot hold when it is weighted, but releasable and moveable without untying when it is unweighted.

Clove Hitch

The clove hitch is used to fasten a rope to a carabiner, tied around the wide base of a carabiner. The beauty of the clove hitch is easy rope-length adjustment without unclipping from the carabiner, making it a truly versatile knot for anchoring purposes: for anchoring a belayer, tying off an anchoring extension rope, or tying off the arms of a cordelette.

Get in the habit of tying the load-bearing strand on the spine side of the carabiner. Doing so loads the carabiner in the strongest configuration. Be sure to tighten the clove hitch properly by cranking down on both strands.

Slip Hitch

This is a simple knot used to tie off a knob or spike of rock.

Munter Hitch

The Munter hitch can be used for belaying, lowering, and rappelling. The mule knot, backed up with an overhand, is used to tie off a Munter hitch. The great advantage of the Munter/mule combination is that it can be tied off and released when the rope is weighted and under tension, making it one of the key knot combinations for many systems used in single pitch terrain.

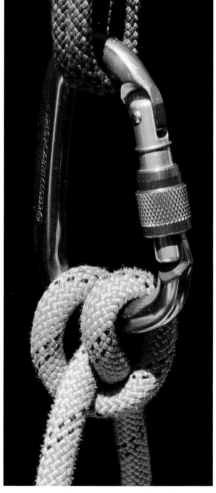

Tying the clove hitch.

How to tie a slip hitch. The slip hitch can be tightened by pulling on one strand, making it more secure than a girth-hitch for tying off knobs of rock.

5

Hold a single strand of rope with both hands, thumbs pointing toward each other.

Cross the right-hand strand in front of the left-hand strand and hold the two strands where they cross with the left thumb and forefinger, then slide the right hand down about 6 inches.

Bring the right strand up and behind the loop.

Clip a locking carabiner where the forefinger is shown here, below the two top strands.

When tying a mule, be aware that when the rope is under tension (holding a climber's weight), it is necessary to maintain control of the brake strand.

Keeping the load and brake strands parallel, form a loop on the brake strand by crossing it behind while still maintaining your grip with your brake hand.

With the non-brake hand, take a bight of rope and pass it through the loop you've created, with the load strand in between the loop and the bight. Snug the mule knot up tight against the Munter hitch.

Pull some slack and finish with an overhand loop backup.

First pass the bight of rope (on the brake hand side) through the belay carabiner.

Then tie the mule knot above your device on the load strand of rope going to the climber.

Finish with an overhand backup.

First pass a bight of rope through the carabiner and form a loop. If the device is under tension, pinching the rope against the device with the opposite hand will help lock it off.

Then pass a bight of rope through the loop you've created, with the spine between the loop and the bight.

Finish by tying an overhand backup on the load strand.

Prusik Knot

A prusik knot is used for rope ascending and as a component in many load transfer systems. It can be loaded in either direction. To tie a prusik, first make a "prusik cord" out of a 5-foot length of 6mm diameter nylon cord tied into a loop with a double fisherman's knot. Buy the softest, most pliable nylon cord available, because a softer cord will grip best. To tie the prusik, simply make a girth-hitch around the rope with the cord, then pass the loop of cord back through the original girth-hitch two or three more times. Dress the knot to make sure all the strands are even and not twisted—a sloppy friction hitch will not grip as well. Test the knot before using it. A thinner cord will grip better, but below 6mm in diameter, the cord will be too weak for many rescue applications. To slide the prusik after it has been weighted, loosen the "tongue," which is the one strand opposite all the wraps.

Tests on various friction hitches reveal that the prusik consistently has the most holding power in a wide array of cord and rope combinations, so use the prusik in scenarios (like 3:1 raising systems) where it will be loaded with more than body weight.

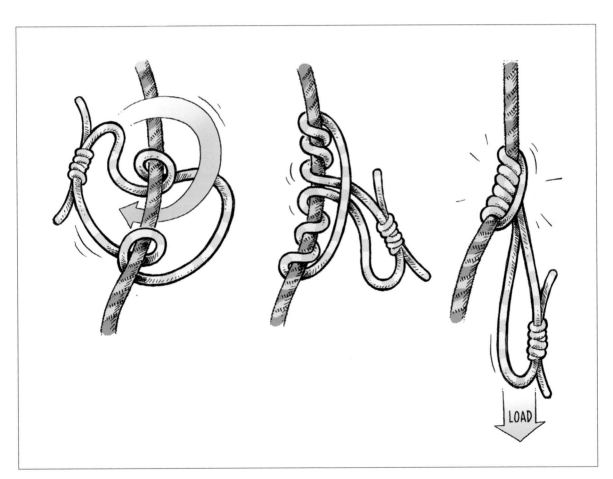

Tying a prusik knot.

A four-wrap prusik.

Klemheist Knot

This is another useful friction hitch that is quick and easy to tie, and is a good choice as a rope-ascending knot or if you're forced to use a sling rather than a piece of cord to tie a friction hitch. If using a sling, pick a nylon one over a Spectra or Dyneema sling, because it grips better and is less susceptible to weakening if it gets hot (nylon has a higher melting point). Four wraps of 6mm cord tied on a single 10mm diameter rope usually work well. After the hitch has been weighted, loosen the tongue (the one strand opposite all the wraps) to slide it more easily. The klemheist also can be loaded in either direction. If tied the opposite way, with the tongue at the base of the wraps, it is commonly referred to as the hedden knot. The hedden knot can be unreliable if it is formed by simply reversing the direction of a klemheist.

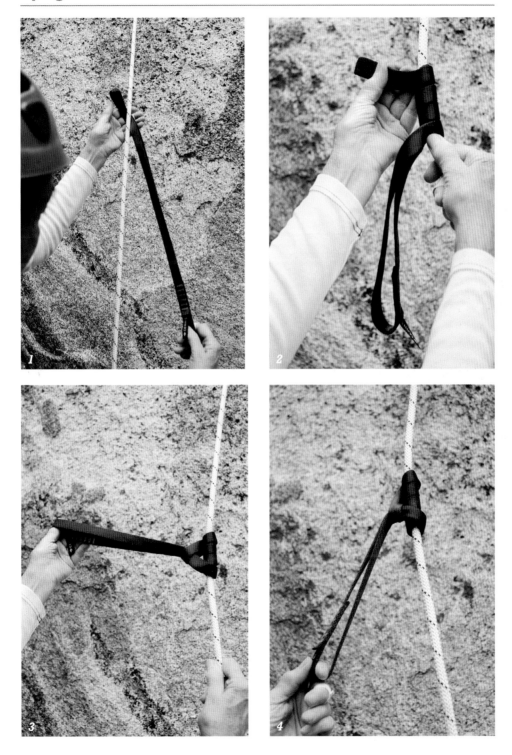

Autoblock

Sometimes called the "third hand," the autoblock is used to back up your brake hand when lowering someone, or to back up the brake hand when rappelling. Tie your autoblock loop from a 4-foot 9-inch length of 5mm- or 6mm-diameter nylon cord tied into a loop with a double fisherman's knot. On a doubled rope, three wraps usually works best, and on a single strand of rope, four wraps.

The autoblock with nylon cord.

The Sterling Hollow Block, shown here wrapped in an autoblock configuration, is a 100 percent Technora sling designed specifically for use with friction hitches.

Stopper Knot

This knot is used as a safety knot in the end of a rope to "close the system." It is essentially half of a triple fisherman's knot tied on one strand of rope. A stopper knot prevents lowering accidents when the rope length is too short and the end of the rope travels through a belay device. A stopper knot also prevents rappelling off the end of the rope if rappelling with a plate, tube, or assisted braking (e.g., Grigri) device. When using two ropes, tie a separate knot at the end of each rope, as tying both ropes together can cause the ropes to twist around each other.

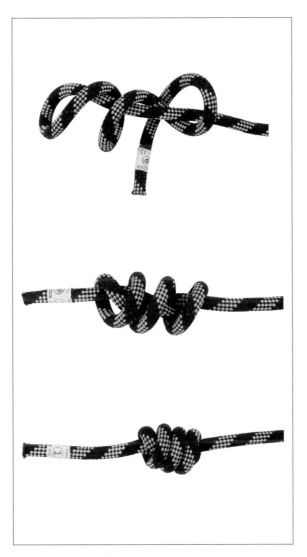

Tying a stopper knot.

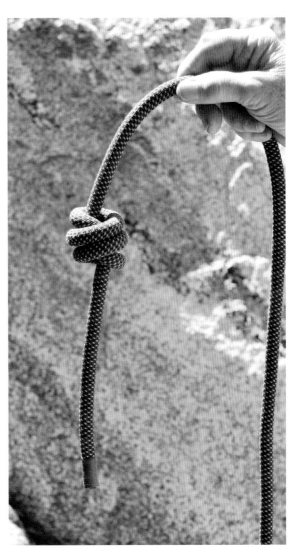

Always close the system by either tying into the end of the rope or tying a stopper knot.

CHAPTER 7

Protection and Anchoring

Nearly every system that a climber can build starts either with good protection placed in solid rock or with strong independent natural features. Many recreational climbers make placements that are "good enough" but could be better. It's an instructor's job to not only make excellent placements, but also to evaluate student placements.

"Good enough" isn't good enough. An instructor should strive to make the best placements possible given the circumstances, while developing strategies to help students understand the dual arts of protecting a climb and building anchors.

Rock Assessment

The first thing to think about when assessing an anchor is the integrity and structure of the rock itself. Catastrophic anchor failures have occurred not because the gear placements were bad, or the rigging was flawed, but because the rock itself was unsound. Determining good rock structure and knowing what to watch out for are fundamental requirements to build solid anchors.

When placing gear, the ideal crack is what instructors call "a crack in the planet," a deep fissure that runs perpendicular (i.e., at a right angle) to the plane of the rock face, cleaving a massive, solid face of granite.

In general, there are two things to avoid: detached blocks and flakes. A detached block is just that—a chunk of rock that is not attached to the main rock structure, but is either sitting on top of the cliff like a boulder, or is part of the main rock face but completely fractured with cracks on all sides.

To assess a block, start by looking at its size. How big is it? Is it the size of a refrigerator, a car, or a house? Putting a piece of gear in the crack beneath a smaller block is a very bad idea. When the piece is weighted, it has a prying effect outward on the block. Even large blocks can shift easily. Look at how the block is situated. Is it perched down low, where it cannot slide out? Does it rest on a flat surface, or is it resting on an inclined slab? When tying off blocks, watch for sharp edges that may fray or cut the rigging rope, and use padding or an edge protector when needed. Generally, be very skeptical of using detached blocks as part of an anchor system, especially smaller blocks.

Flakes should also be avoided. A flake is formed by a crack in the rock that runs parallel to the main rock face. It can be wafer thin, or several feet thick. A flake is inherently weak, since any gear placement, when loaded, will exert a prying effect outward on the structure of the flake, which can fracture the flake if it's not strong enough to bear the force. In a naturally weak rock, like sandstone, a thin flake of rock can be extremely weak.

Exfoliation is a natural process of granite formations and is the key in the formation of domes. Flakes of granite are layered, like layers of an onion, and the outer layer peels off from time to time due to the effects of weathering and gravity, exposing a new layer beneath.

Use good judgment if anchoring to detached blocks. Avoid small ones and those situated on an inclined slab or those precariously perched. A good rule of thumb when using detached blocks is this: for a sole monolithic anchor, the block should be at least as big as a full-sized refrigerator, resting on a flat surface.

Rockslide!

One of the largest examples of exfoliation occurred in Yosemite Valley on a hot July day in 1996 at the Glacier Point Apron. An enormous flake, roughly the size of a football field and about 4 feet thick, detached from a point high on the cliff, shearing off in one gigantic piece. After a 2,000-foot free fall, the impact resulted in a massive explosion, creating a 300 mile per hour shock wave of wind that felled a thousand pine trees in a wide swath. A tourist, in line at the Happy Isles snack bar over a quarter mile away, was killed when hit by a piece of the shrapnel from the blast.

This camming device has been placed behind a flake of rock (left). If the cam is loaded, it will pry outward, potentially breaking the flake. This can cause the anchor to fail and also send the chunk of rock tumbling down onto people below.

This fabricated anchor is set up only to illustrate a point. Leaning back on this rappel anchor would most likely pull this detached flake right off the cliff.

When building anchors, look with skepticism at any flake. How thick is it, and how well attached to the main rock structure or cliff face? Test its soundness by thumping on it with the palm of the hand.

Does it vibrate? Is there a hollow sound? When analyzing rock structure, act like a geologist and scrutinize the rock and its various formations very carefully.

Another dangerous anchor rig using a very questionable block. The block sits on a severely inclined slab, and a pull on this toprope anchor setup may be just enough to send it sliding down the slab and over the brink.

Macro to Micro Rock Assessment

When assessing rock structure, evaluate from macro to micro. Macro is the big picture. Look at the main rock face. Is there a massive, solid rock structure? Is there a crack in the planet? Or are the cracks an intricate matrix where no real massive piece of completely solid rock exists. Are there block or flakes? Is it possible to avoid using them? These are questions

This detached flake is a great example of bad rock structure.

that need to be asked. Never blindly place gear in cracks without first scrutinizing the big picture: the overall structure and integrity of the rock itself.

Microstructure is what's inside the crack. Is the surface of the rock rotten, grainy, dirty, or flaky? Are there hollow spots or hollow flakes inside the crack itself? Microstructure can affect the integrity of gear placements as much as the overall macrostructure.

Bad microstructure: The right side of this nut rests on a fragile flake.

You don't have to be a geologist to figure out that this flake is ready to exfoliate. Many catastrophic anchor failures are due to poor rock structure.

Natural Anchors

Natural anchors utilize the natural features found at the crag environment, such as trees, and the configuration of the rock itself. Trees are plentiful in some areas, rare in others, like in a desert environment. When assessing the reliability of a tree, there are several considerations. Is the tree alive or dead? What is the environment (dry or wet)? What is the diameter of the tree's trunk? How deeply rooted is the tree? When using a tree as part of an anchor system, a good rule of thumb is to choose a live, healthy tree with a minimum trunk diameter of approximately 12 inches. Generally speaking, trees rooted in a thin carpet of topsoil tend to be less reliable as anchor points than those deeply rooted in a thicker layer of topsoil. Climate should also be taken into account when considering the use of trees as anchor points. Trees in areas where the climate is wet and humid and the topsoil is thin can be less desirable as anchors than those in an area of thin topsoil but a dry climate.

The rock itself can be used for anchoring. Look for large spikes or horns of rock attached to the main rock structure to tie off as part of the anchor. A tunnel in a solid rock structure is called a thread and is utilized by threading a sling or cord, or tying a rope, through the tunnel. Limestone is a rock type with many threads, whereas threads in granite are a rarity.

OK. A properly girth-hitched nylon sling.

Good. A double-length (48-inch) nylon sling tied with an overhand knot makes the sling itself redundant.

Good. A figure eight follow-through knot used to tie the anchor rope directly to the tree.

I (BG) came across this natural anchor several hundred feet up a route on Tahquitz Rock, near Idyllwild, California. Someone had obviously rappelled from it, probably to escape an afternoon thunderstorm. Although the anchor has two basic components, each trunk is less than 3 inches in diameter, and the master point where you'd thread your rappel rope is a nonredundant, single aluminum rappel ring (albeit rated at 3,000 lbs.). The real problem I have with this rappel anchor is simply the size of the "tree" itself. I'm glad I didn't have to rappel from it!

A solid block tied off with a doubled cordelette using a figure eight knot, making the cordelette itself redundant.

A sling threaded through a tunnel with a girth-hitch. This is called a "thread."

The same thread with a doubled cordelette tied with a figure eight. This adds redundancy—if one loop is cut, three loops back it up.

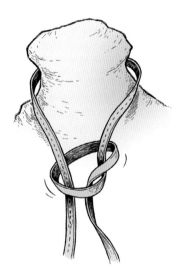
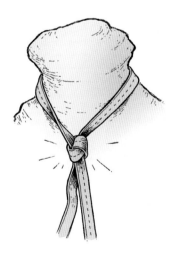

A slip hitch used to tie off a knob of rock.

Monolithic Anchors

Instructors will often encounter natural anchors that are so large and reliable, they may be trusted as the sole component in an anchoring system. Titanic boulders and large trees are often unquestionably reliable, and that level of absolute certainty is how the merit of a monolith should be evaluated. If, after careful examination and consideration, there is any doubt of the integrity, security, and strength of a monolithic component, it is not monolithic and should not be used, or should be backed up appropriately. Common examples include living, deeply rooted trees that are larger in diameter than

A single pine tree used for a toprope anchor. Both the cord and the carabiners are doubled for redundancy in the rigging.

the entire climbing team; or a boulder the size of a small vehicle, firmly attached and embedded in the landscape.

Just make sure the sling or rope around the anchor is redundant. For example, when rigging a rappel anchor around a tree, use two separate slings with two rappel rings to gain redundancy in the anchor system, at least in the rigging. When rigging a belay or toprope anchor, loop two strands of the cordelette around the tree, then tie a figure eight knot for a two-loop master point. Clip in with two locking carabiners, opposed and reversed, to achieve redundancy in the anchor rigging (although technically, one single tree is nonredundant). Use caution and sound judgment when using a nonredundant natural anchor.

Passive Protection

The Evolution of Chockcraft

A chockstone is simply a rock wedged in a crack. Naturally occurring chockstones can be as small as a pebble or as big as a house. The notion of using a chockstone for an anchor dates back to the origins of the sport. In the late 1800s, in the British Isles, rock climbers began using natural chockstones for anchors by slinging a cord around them and attaching their rope to the sling with a carabiner. The use of artificial chockstones—called chocks, or more commonly, nuts—began in the early 1960s, at a cliff in North Wales of all places, at a crag named Clogwyn du'r Arddu. The hike up to the crag followed a railroad track, and some ambling climber picked up a nut along the way and pocketed it. Up on the cliff he threaded a small cord through the nut before wedging it in a constriction in a thin crack. Thus the subtle art of chockcraft was born.

In American rock climbing, pitons were used almost exclusively for protection and anchors until the 1970s. In Europe, pitons were made of soft iron and once hammered into a crack were nearly impossible to remove and reuse. Legendary

A selection of chocks from the 1970s. Nuts have evolved over the years but are still based on the same original basic designs.

Now You See It, Now You Don't

A friend of mine (BG) put up a new route at Joshua Tree—a 40-foot-high sport climb with five bolts—up the face of a massive block that was a facet of a larger cliff. One day I got a phone call: "Tony's route fell down!" I didn't believe it until I walked out there and saw it with my own eyes. The gigantic block was top heavy and had simply toppled over, with the side where Tony's route was now straight down in the dirt, leaving behind a void in the cliff the size of a small house. I got down on my hands and knees and peered underneath. I could see one of the bolt hangers! Bouldering legend Chris Sharma visited the site shortly thereafter, climbing what is now one of Joshua Tree's most difficult boulder problems, up the newly exposed overhanging face of one side of the block.

A selection of modern-day nuts.

American climber John Salathe, a wrought-iron worker by trade, developed the first hard steel pitons, forged from an old Ford Model A axle, which he used for his famous ascents in Yosemite Valley during the 1940s. These high carbon steel pitons could be driven and then removed, over and over again.

Yvon Chouinard refined and innovated the design of chrome molly steel pitons from 1957 to 1965, improving on Salathe's designs with the introduction of knifeblade, horizontal (called the Lost Arrow), and angle pitons. These pitons revolutionized big wall climbing in Yosemite during the "Golden Age" of the 1960s, where hundreds of placements were required for the ultimate big wall climbs in Yosemite, like El Capitan. Once placed, they could be removed by the second, leaving the climbing route in the same condition for the next climbing team. Climbing standards in Yosemite led the world at the time.

But it came with a price. On popular climbs in Yosemite, the repeated pounding and removal of hard steel pitons began to permanently damage the cracks, leaving ugly "pin scars" every few feet up

*Piton scars on a
Yosemite crack.*

crack systems. Cracks were getting "beat out," and something had to be done. In Yosemite the National Park Service actually closed down a few climbs because of piton damage.

When the great American climber Royal Robbins made a trip to England in the 1960s, he saw how effective nuts could be, and he imported the idea back to Yosemite. His 1967 ascent of The Nutcracker, one of Yosemite's most popular climbs, was done entirely with nuts, Royal's way of showing that nuts were a viable alternative to the destructive pitons. Today there still are piton scars on the route, a testament to how slow American climbers were to embrace the new and more gentle technology of chockcraft—a big change from bashing hard steel pitons into cracks with heavy blows from a hammer.

The change was finally precipitated by the fact that many cracks were simply being destroyed. Even granite is relatively soft when compared to cold hard steel. But it wasn't until Yvon Chouinard introduced chocks to American rock climbers in

his 1972 equipment catalog, and Doug Robinson espoused the virtues of nuts in his seminal treatise, *The Whole Natural Art of Protection,* that the American climbing community firmly embraced the idea of "clean climbing," a new ethic where climbing anchors were placed and removed without scarring or damaging the rock.

Today there are thin crack climbs in Yosemite where for hundreds of feet every finger jam is in an ancient piton scar, although now instead of using pitons, nuts can be slotted into the V-shaped bottom of the old pin scars.

Artificial chocks now come in a dazzling array of shapes and sizes, the largest ones capable of holding over 3,000 pounds, and the tiniest micro-nuts designed to hold body weight only. The Hexentric, commonly called a Hex, is a unique, six-sided nut with four distinct orientations of placement, first introduced by Chouinard Equipment in 1971. It was followed by the Stopper in 1972, with its simple, but effective, tapered trapezoidal shape. Although there have been many new designs

The classic designs of the Hex (left) and the Stopper (right) have changed little since their inception in the early 1970s.

introduced since then, they are basically variations on a theme to these classic and timeless designs, which are still as viable today as they were more than forty years ago.

Another ingenious design, called the Tricam, invented by Greg Lowe in 1973 and available to the public in 1981, is essentially a single cam that can be used either passively or actively. Since it has a tapered design, with a point on one end, it can be wedged like a nut (called a passive placement) or used like a cam (called an active placement), where a mechanical action (i.e., camming) takes place. The camming action occurs when the sling is loaded on the back, or spine, of the cam, between two rails that contact the rock on one side of the crack, creating a force that pivots like a fulcrum onto the

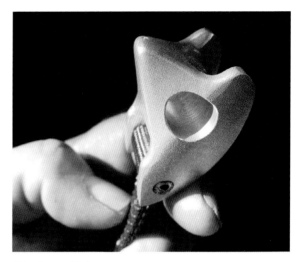

The Lowe Tricam.

Tricam in camming mode.

Tricam in passive mode.

To assess a nut placement, remember these three key elements:

1. Rock structure
2. Direction of pull
3. Surface contact

A good acronym is SOS:

S Structural integrity of the rock

O Orientation (direction of pull)

S Surface contact

obvious constrictions in the crack itself. A "bottleneck" placement is found where the crack tapers drastically, and the proper size nut is fitted in the narrowing constriction.

With a basic tapered nut, like the Stopper, the preferred placement is in the narrow configuration, since this setting has the most surface contact and stability. The wider endwise configuration is an option for narrow slots and shallow cracks, but ultimately has less surface contact and generally less stability.

The typical nut placement is in a vertical crack, but horizontal cracks will work if there is a narrowing at the lip of the crack and you can slide a nut in

pointed end on the other side of the crack. The design is useful for many horizontal crack situations, but can be somewhat difficult to remove with one hand or once it is weighted.

Be aware that in the smaller-size Tricams, when set in the passive mode, a Stopper of similar size is considerably stronger. The reason is because on the Tricam, the load is being placed directly on the scroll pin that connects the webbing to the body of the Tricam. (A pink Tricam in passive mode is rated at 6 kN; a similarly sized Stopper, 10 kN. In camming mode the pink Tricam is rated at 9 kN.)

When placing a nut, or any other piece of gear for that matter, again the first thing to consider is the overall integrity of the rock itself. The importance of rock assessment cannot be overemphasized. Nuts have very low holding power in soft sandstone, rotten, or flaky rock. Avoid placing nuts in cracks under or around detached blocks, or in cracks behind loose flakes. Look for "straight-in" cracks in massive rock structure, where the crack runs perpendicular to the plane of the rock face.

Once a good crack system is found, look for

Stopper in a bottleneck placement. There is simply no way that in a downward pull the nut could be pulled through the bottleneck—something would have to give, either the rock itself or the nut or wire cable breaking.

from the side, then pull it into the constriction.

The real art of chockcraft comes into play with the more subtle placements. Look for any slight variations in the walls of the crack. When placing a nut, aim for maximum surface contact between the metal faces of the chock and the walls of the crack.

When the walls of the crack are virtually parallel sided, using the camming action of a Tricam or Hex is the best option for a nut placement, although this is territory that specific camming devices were designed for.

After rock quality has been assessed, the next concern when placing a nut is the direction of pull.

In what direction will the chock be loaded? Most placements can withstand a pull in only *one* direction. While the nut may be able to withstand a load of 2,000 pounds in that one direction, the slightest tug in the opposite direction might jerk the nut right out of its placement. When incorporating a nut placement into an overall anchor system, look at the ultimate direction the anchor system will be loaded and orient placements in a line toward this focal point (called the master point).

Setting a nut properly is also important. Many novice climbers make a great nut placement but fail to set it properly, which makes the nut susceptible

Excellent. This Stopper placement is in good, solid rock and has flush surface contact on both sides of the nut.

Good. This endwise Stopper placement has good surface contact on both sides.

Bad. The left side of this nut lacks surface contact with the rock.

Marginal. This Stopper is in a good bottleneck, but since it lacks flush contact on the right side, a slightly outward pull will pluck it from its placement.

Good. The left side of this nut is nearly 100 percent flush, and the curve of the nut on its right side fits the curve of the crack.

Excellent. This nut has good surface contact on both sides, plus the lip on the right side of the crack protects against any outward force.

Excellent. This Hex placement has near complete contact on both faces of the nut in a solid straight-in crack. Loading the nut's cable will kick in the camming action of the Hex.

to levering out of its placement if pulled from a different angle than intended. Setting the piece is accomplished by simply applying several stout tugs in the direction the piece will be loaded, most easily accomplished by attaching a sling to the nut with a carabiner and yanking on the sling, firmly wedging the nut in its intended placement. While this definitely makes the nut more difficult to remove, it is an important concept that many novices miss.

Carrying a nut tool, which is a metal pick designed for nut removal, facilitates "cleaning" nuts. To clean a nut can be as easy as yanking it in the opposite direction from the intended direction of pull, but be careful with recalcitrant nuts that can

suddenly pop out and hit your face or teeth. Yanking a piece out can also send a hand bashing into the rock, scraping knuckles. A better approach to removing a nut is to use the nut tool, giving the nut a tap opposite from the direction of loading. For larger nuts an easy way to loosen them is to tap the nut with a carabiner, metal to metal.

To become skilled at chockcraft takes practice. Look for good rock structure, preferably a straight-in crack. Then look for any obvious V-shaped constrictions in the crack. If there is nothing obvious, look for any subtle narrowing of the width of the crack. Practice nut placements, aiming for maximum surface contact between metal and rock, keeping in

Good. This Hex is in a narrowing pocket, and both sides of the nut have good surface contact.

Bad. No surface contact on the left side makes this Hex placement likely to fail with the slightest outward force.

Excellent. This endwise placement has great surface contact on both sides.

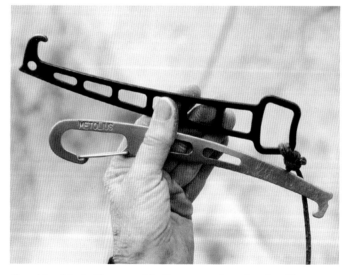

A nut tool is indispensable for removing chocks. Here are two models: Black Diamond (top) and Metolius (bottom).

To remove a nut with a nut tool, Inspect the placement and determine the intended direction of pull, then tap in the opposite direction.

mind the paramount importance of direction of pull. Set the nut with a sharp tug. Once set, it should not move, pivot, or wiggle in its placement when you test it with a slight tug in the opposite direction of the intended direction of loading. Practice will help to develop the knack for seeing what size nut is needed for a particular placement, then selecting the proper nut and fitting it into the crack on the first try. Every nut placement is different, some less than perfect, some great, some worthless. It is important to have enough knowledge to know what's good and what's not, and what constitutes a placement that can be trusted.

Active Protection

In the mid-1970s a stout, muscular fellow by the name of Ray Jardine could often be seen peering through binoculars, gazing upward at the various nooks and crannies on the walls of Yosemite Valley. With his thick beard and glasses, he looked like a bird watcher, but Ray wasn't looking for birds. The bulging forearms gave it away—Ray was a climber, and he was looking for the ultimate crack: one of those perfectly straight cracks that split Yosemite's steep walls like a surgeon's incision, shooting upward for a hundred feet, uninterrupted.

Ray had invented a new technology—the spring-loaded camming device, or SLCD—that allowed him to place reliable protection in even perfectly parallel-sided cracks. When he found his ultimate crack climb, he swore his partners to secrecy and set out on a mission: to climb the most difficult crack ever climbed in Yosemite. He named it the *Phoenix*—a fingertip to hand-size crack on a gently overhanging wall high above Cascade Falls in the lower valley. After dozens of attempts using his new-fangled technology, he finally succeeded in climbing Yosemite's first 5.13. Ray called his miracle invention the "Friend," and soon the word was out. Some climbers called it "cheating," while others claimed it was "the greatest invention since the nylon rope."

Marketed by Wild Country, the Friend soon became an integral part of every rock climber's rack. Ray soon retired from climbing and, financed by his proceeds from the licensing of the Friend, went on to sail around the world, hike the Pacific Crest Trail, row across the Atlantic, and ski to the South Pole.

The idea of the SLCD, or "camming device" for short, is simple in concept yet complex in design. Jardine's original design consisted of a unit with a rigid aluminum shaft connected by an axle to four independent, spring-loaded aluminum cams (called "lobes"). The cams retracted via a trigger bar that slid up and down a slot in the shaft. The unit was fitted into a parallel-sided crack with the cams retracted; when weight was applied to a sling tied

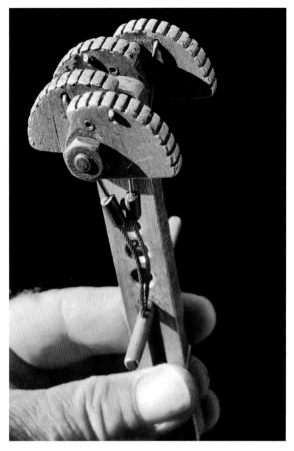

The original Wild Country Friend was one of the greatest innovations in rock climbing.

Spring-loaded camming devices have become an integral part of every climber's rack.

into a hole in the bottom of the shaft, the cams were activated in response to the load. To keep the unit from being pulled out of the crack, a corresponding force held it in place. The downward force in the direction of the shaft was transferred outward at the cams, which generated an outward force against the walls of the crack.

The disadvantage of Ray's design was that a rigid shaft could not flex or bend in the direction of pull, an especially troubling problem for placements in horizontal cracks.

Today there is a huge array of SLCDs on the market, and the majority of these designs have flexible wire cable shafts instead of rigid ones. One of the biggest improvements since the invention of the Friend was the first double-axle design, called the Camalot, introduced by Black Diamond Equipment, which allows for a much greater range of placement of the cams. Now, in addition to units with four cam lobes, there are TCUs (three-cam units) and offset cams (for flared cracks).

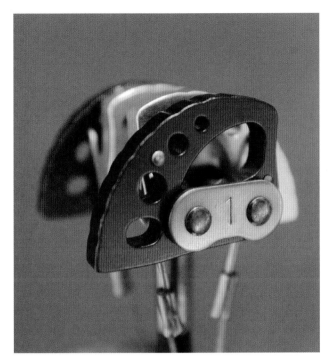

The Black Diamond Camalot was the first double-axle design.

The Metolius Power Cam has color-coded dots that help you assess your placement.

The Metolius offset TCU (three-cam unit) works well in slightly flaring cracks.

Placing an SLCD

When placing an SLCD, the first thing to consider is rock quality. SLCDs can fail if the rock is soft, brittle, or loose. They can easily pull out if placed behind a small, loose block or thin flake of rock. In solid granite, in an ideal placement, a Black Diamond Camalot can hold as much as 14 kN (3,147 lbs.) Do not rely on a camming device to hold in very soft sandstone, or in rotten or flaky rock. Cam manufacturer Metolius advises: "Rock fails in two basic ways: either a relatively large piece breaks off

Bad. Any force applied to this Black Diamond Camalot will be converted to an outward force that can pry out and potentially break the flake of rock it's placed behind.

or the surface layer is crushed under the pressure of the cam lobe, allowing the cam to 'track out.' Instructors must assess the integrity of the rock and choose the soundest possible location for your placements. Look for fractures in and around the walls of a potential placement that could denote weakness, as well as pebbles, crystals, or micro-flakes that could snap off. Be extremely suspicious of placements behind flakes or blocks."

Since they rely on friction to a certain extent, camming devices are not as strong in exceptionally slick or polished rock, or rock that is wet or icy. Again, avoid placements behind detached blocks and loose flakes—the outward expansion of the cams can generate a tremendous force that can pry the rock loose. Look for straight-in cracks in solid rock. A straight-in crack is one that runs perpendicular to the face of the rock, bisecting the rock at a right angle.

When placing a camming device, look for a section of the crack where the walls are uniformly parallel, or where they form a subtle pocket. Avoid widening cracks, where the crack is wider above the cams, as the camming device, due to its spring-loaded design, will naturally have a tendency to wiggle upward as the cam is activated. This phenomenon is known as "walking." This walking movement is most exaggerated when the cam's sling and cable are manipulated from side to side, but it can also happen when the piece is repeatedly weighted and unweighted, as in toproping. In a crack where the walls are uniformly parallel, or where the crack narrows slightly above the cams, if there is any walking, the cams will not open any wider and will stay within acceptable retraction range. As a test, pull the device from side to side to see what walking, if any, occurs. There is only one definitive solution to walking: Cams must be placed in a slot or crack that dead-ends or closes off. Otherwise, walking can be somewhat mitigated by slinging, supervising the placement, and creating anchor systems that self-adjust as direction of load

Bad. Even though the cams on this Black Diamond Camalot are within the acceptable range (right around 50 percent retracted), the widening crack above will allow the cams to easily "walk" into the wider section, even with minimal loading and unloading of the device. Avoid this situation, since the cams can potentially walk to an open and unstable position.

Very good placement. All the cams have good surface contact in a solid, straight-in crack, and the cams are in the recommended range for a Camalot (50 to 90 percent retraction).

varies. The key point here is that walking is something to be aware of and watch for.

Another key to a good placement is the range of retraction on the cams. Black Diamond recommends that the Camalot be placed in the lower to mid-expansion range (50 to 90 percent retraction), while Wild Country advises the following for its single-axle designs: "It is vitally important that all the cams make contact with the sides of the rock, preferably in the middle half of their expansion range (i.e., the cams should be one-quarter to three-quarters open)." Metolius recommends to "select the largest size cam that will fit without getting stuck. Cams should not be placed near the wide end of their expansion range. When a unit is loaded, it expands as the slack is removed from the system and the cams and rock compress. A nearly tipped-out cam won't have enough expansion left to accommodate this process. A loose cam is also more prone to walking and has little range left to adjust."

Bad. The two outside cams are not in the acceptable range for a Camalot (too wide), and they don't have flush contact with the walls of the crack.

Good. This Metolius Power Cam displays optimal green "range finder" dots in a solid, parallel-sided crack.

Poor. Although the range of retraction is acceptable, this Metolius Power Cam could easily walk up into the wider pod in the crack above the cams, rendering the placement unstable. Also, the outside right cam has poor surface contact and is too close to the edge of the crack.

Placing a camming device with a rigid shaft in a horizontal crack with the shaft protruding can be dangerous because the shaft can break if loaded at a 90-degree angle during a leader fall.

Camming units with flexible shafts are the best option for horizontal placement. Metolious recommends that in a horizontal crack, the outside cams should be placed on the bottom of the crack for maximum stability.

Good. This Camalot, placed in a solid horizontal slot, has all four cams tighter than 50 percent retraction with flush surface contact.

Borderline too tight. This Camalot is around 90 percent retracted. Any tighter and it may be very difficult to remove. There is also some loss of holding power in the last 10 percent (90 to 100 percent retracted) on a Camalot.

Very poor. The cams are barely retracted and nowhere near the recommended range. The piece can easily walk and might fail completely.

Borderline marginal. While this Metolius Power Cam is in a pocket that lends some stability to the placement, the range of retraction is between the yellow and red "range finder" dots; the red dots signify a marginal placement. The next larger unit would fit nicely.

Fair. This Camalot is in a slightly flaring crack, with the inside cams retracted tighter than the outside ones, although each set of cams (inside and outside) are within a suitable range and all the cams have flush contact with the rock.

Bad. The crack is way too flared for this Metolius Power Cam, and the cam on the right side has very poor surface contact with the rock.

Good. This Metolius cam is in the tighter aspect of its range. Green means good to go.

Bad. The cams are too open, rendering the placement unstable. Shoot for at least halfway tight on the cams.

The same crack with two different placements. In the left-hand photo, the left outside cam has poor contact and is too close to the edge of the crack. By flipping the cam around (right photo), the gold cam now has flush surface contact with the rock. Since the inside and outside sets of cams are offset, flipping the cam one way or the other can often afford a better placement, particularly in shallow cracks in corners.

To illustrate what constitutes an acceptable range of retraction for the cams of a camming device, let's look at the Black Diamond Camalot in greater detail.

What is 50 to 90 percent retracted for a double-axle camming device like the Camalot? When you're looking at the Camalot without pulling on the trigger, it's at 0 percent retraction. Squeezing the trigger mechanism so that the cams are as tight as possible is 100 percent retracted. At 100 percent retracted, in a very tight placement, the Camalot will likely be very difficult to remove. In the last

10 percent of the tightest aspect of the range (90 to 100 percent retracted), the Camalot also loses some of its holding power, another reason not to go too tight on a placement. The starting point for a good placement is at 50 percent retraction, which is when the cams are pulled at least halfway tight. Looking at the base of the cams, 50 percent retraction is when the base of each cam is at a 45-degree angle relative to the vertical axis of the Camalot. If the cams are symmetrically retracted, they will be at a 90-degree angle relative to each other. A common mistake is to place a Camalot near the outer limit

The innovative Link Cam, by Omega Pacific, covers the range of four standard camming devices in a single unit.

of its range (0 to 50 percent retraction). This can prove to be a very unstable placement if the unit moves at all in the crack, which can easily happen if the Camalot is placed in a crack that widens above the cams and the piece is repeatedly weighted and unweighted. Again, the optimal Camalot placement is when the cams are at least halfway tight (50 percent retracted). From the beginning position, pull the trigger mechanism until the range on the cams is half the starting size, then go only smaller and tighter from there. Scrutinize your placement after the camming device has been placed in a crack to make sure the cams are in the acceptable range.

Metolius cams have a unique color coding that assists in their assessment. The company gives this advice: "Verify that you have chosen the best size by making sure that the green Range Finder dots are lined up where the cam lobes touch the walls of the placement. Yellow dot alignment is okay too, but you must exercise more caution with the placement, because the cam will be less stable, hence more prone to walking, and it will have less expansion range left to accommodate walking to a wider position. If the cam you choose aligns in the yellow zone, the next larger size will align perfectly in the green zone. Use that cam instead, if it's still on your rack. Never use a placement in the red zone unless it's the only placement available."

Study the literature that comes with any camming device and learn what the manufacturer recommends for the acceptable range of retraction and the various placement criteria. Most manufacturers also have informative PDF files on camming device guidelines that can be downloaded from the company's website.

To become proficient in the use of camming devices takes thought and practice. To develop confidence quickly, hire an AMGA certified guide or climbing instructor to critique placements. Metolius suggests to "practice placing cams in a safe venue,

Ground Practice

Whint I (BG) teach camming device placements, I first demonstrate the fundamentals, then let students make a variety of placements with a critique on each one. Working with an instructor allows them to learn from their mistakes before venturing out on their own. Better to learn in a "ground-school" setting than on their first toprope anchor that their "Friend" was no friend at all.

at ground level, before you trust your life to a cam placement. This process can teach you a lot, but written guidelines and practice are no substitute for qualified instruction. We strongly recommend that you learn to place cams under the supervision of a certified guide."

Fixed Anchors

Pitons

A piton is a metal spike that is hammered into a crack for an anchor. The blade of the piton is the part hammered into the crack, leaving the

protruding eye into which a carabiner can be clipped. Piton anchors are something of a rarity these days, but occasionally fixed pitons (also called pins) can be found at the top of a crag. Follow these steps before using any fixed pin. First, assess the rock structure and look at the crack where the piton resides. Is it behind a block or flake, or is it in a straight-in crack with good structure? A good piton should be driven in all the way to the eye, and should not wiggle when clipping into it with a sling and pulling on it to test it. The piton itself should not be excessively corroded or cracked. (Look closely at the eye of the piton, as this is usually where the piton will be cracked.) To effectively

Pitons (left to right):
Angle, horizontal, Leeper
Z, knifeblade.

An angle piton, driven all the way to the eye—a good placement.

test a fixed pin, a hammer is needed. Give the piton a light tap—it should have a high-pitched ring to it, and the hammer should spring off the piton. Without a hammer, tap it with a carabiner or small rock. The best test is to clip a sling into it and give it a vigorous yank in the direction it will be loaded. Over time, pitons suffer from the vagaries of thermal expansion and contraction, particularly in winter, as water expands when it freezes, prying and loosening the piton. Often a piton can be easily plucked out by hand after only a few seasons. If utilizing fixed pitons as part of a toprope anchor system, always back them up, and use them with skepticism.

Bolts

The most common fixed anchor is a two-bolt anchor. Some knowledge of the history, characteristics, and specifications of bolts used for rock climbing will improve one's ability to assess the reliability of bolt anchors.

In the 1960s and 1970s, bolts were placed by hand drilling—an arduous process where a drill bit was inserted into a drill holder, then a hammer was used to pound on the holder to painstakingly drill into the rock. Once the hole was deep enough, a bolt, with a hanger attached, was hammered into the hole. The most common bolt during that era was the ubiquitous ¼-inch contraction bolt, called the Rawl Drive, manufactured by the Rawl Company and designed for the construction industry for anchoring in masonry or concrete. A contraction bolt has a split shaft that is wider than the diameter of the hole. When pounded into the hole, the two bowed shaft pieces are forced to straighten slightly, contracting under tension in the hole. This works fine for hard granite, but in soft rock, like sandstone, the split shaft doesn't really contract all that much, and there is little tension to keep it in the hole, resulting in very weak pullout strength (i.e., pulling straight out on the bolt).

Another problem with ¼-inch bolts is that they came in various lengths, some as short as ¾ inch long, and once placed in the rock, there was no way for future climbers to determine the length of the bolt merely by inspection.

There are two basic styles of ¼-inch Rawl Drive bolts. The buttonhead design has a mushroom-like head and is pounded into the hole with the hanger preattached. The threaded Rawl Drive has threads with a nut on the end to hold the hanger in place, a weaker configuration since the threads can weaken the shear strength of the shaft if the hanger is at the level of the threads. But more significantly, the threaded design has a serious flaw: Pulling straight out on the bolt hanger will only be as strong as the holding power of the nut on the threads, a dangerous problem if the nut is at the very end of the threads.

The shear strength on a brand-new ¼-inch Rawl Drive bolt is roughly 2,000 pounds, but the problem with contraction bolts is not shear strength but pullout strength, which varies drastically depending on the quality and hardness of the rock. In very soft sandstone the pullout strength of a ¼-inch contraction bolt is extremely low, rendering the bolt unsafe.

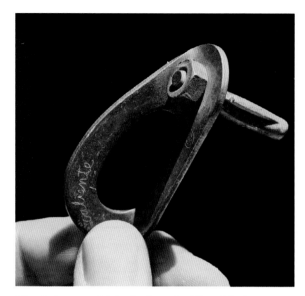

The infamous ¼-inch threaded Rawl Drive contraction bolt, complete with the SMC "death hanger." This ticking time bomb was removed and replaced from a route on Suicide Rock, California.

Buttonhead Rawl Drive contraction bolts (left to right): ⅜-, ⁵⁄₁₆-, and ¼-inch sizes.

The buttonhead Rawl Drive bolts were also sold in ⁵⁄₁₆-inch diameters, these being far more reliable as long as they were placed in good, hard, fine-grained granite. The ⁵⁄₁₆-inch buttonhead, for example, has a shear and pullout strength in excess of 4,000 pounds, and for many years was the bolt of choice for first ascensionists who were hand drilling bolts. The ⁵⁄₁₆-inch buttonhead Rawl Drive was discontinued, but the ⅜-inch buttonhead is still on the market today, with a shear strength of 7,000 pounds and a pullout strength of over 4,000 pounds in the best granite.

Probably the most disconcerting problem associated with bolts from the ¼-inch era is not the bolts themselves but the hangers. During that time, hangers made for rock climbing were manufactured primarily by the SMC company. Thankfully, the hangers are easily identified, as the "SMC" brand is stamped on them. There were two series of hangers: one good, and one very bad. The "bad" hangers

¼-inch threaded Rawl Drive bolts with "good" (left) versus "bad" (right) SMC hangers.

⁵⁄₁₆-inch buttonhead Rawl contraction bolt with "good" SMC hanger. In a good placement in solid granite, these bolts are rated at over 4,000 pounds shear strength.

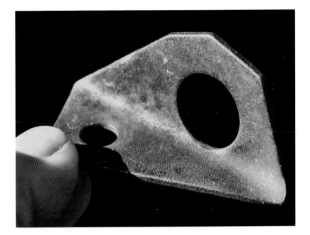

The recalled Leeper hanger can easily be identified by its unique shape and rusty condition.

Bad corrosion on a ³⁄₈-inch diameter threaded Rawl Drive bolt with a badly corroded Leeper hanger to match.

were nicknamed the SMC "death hangers," since some of them failed under body weight after only a few seasons of exposure to the elements. These hangers are identifiable by a distinctive corrosive discoloration—a yellowish or bronze tint, whereas the "good" SMC hangers, made from stainless steel, show no signs of corrosion or rust and still appear silvery bright, even after twenty-five years. Another noticeable difference is in the thickness of the hangers—the "bad" hangers roughly the thickness of a dime, and the "good" ones the thickness of a quarter.

Another dangerous relic from the 1970s is the Leeper hanger. Over 9,000 of these hangers were manufactured by Ed Leeper of Colorado, and subsequently recalled because of stress corrosion

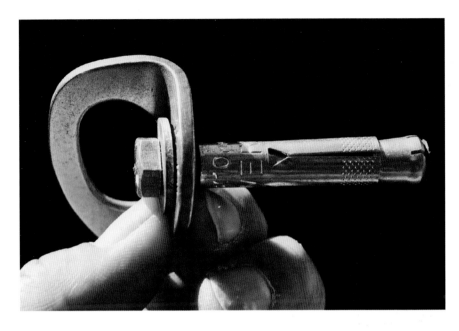

The ⅜-inch diameter Powers Power Bolt expansion bolt with a stainless steel hanger has become the minimum standard for climbing anchor bolts.

problems with the metal, which rusted badly since it was not made of stainless steel. These hangers are easily identifiable due to their strange geometric shape and their rusty condition.

In the 1980s sport climbing was ushered into the United States, and climbers began to place bolts on rappel using cordless rotary hammer power drills. Since these bolts would now have to absorb numerous falls, climbers began to look for the strongest bolts available, and the standard became ⅜-inch diameter for good, solid rock (like granite) and ½-inch diameter for softer rock (like sandstone)—standards that are still prevalent today.

Although there are numerous types of bolts used in rock climbing today, the gold standard has long been the "5-piece Rawl" expansion bolt (now sold as the Powers Power Bolt). This expansion bolt has a shaft with a hex head on one end and threads on the other end (the end that goes in the hole), with a cone-shaped piece screwed onto the threads. The shaft has a two-part split sleeve, and as the hex head is tightened, the cone climbs up the threads and under the sleeves, which presses the sleeves outward, "expanding" the bolt in the hole. The more

you tighten it, the wider the sleeve gets. The performance and strength of the bolt relies, to a great extent, on two things: the tolerance (diameter) of the hole, and the strength of the rock itself. In good rock the ⅜-inch Power Bolt is rated at over 7,000 pounds shear strength, with a pullout strength of roughly 5,000 pounds.

Since these bolts are really designed for the construction business, the Powers Fastener company lists strength ratings based on the density of the concrete they are placed in. Concrete is given a psi (pounds per square inch) rating. For example, "2,000 psi concrete" means that it would take a weight of 2,000 pounds to crush a square inch of concrete. Hard, dense granite is analogous to 6,000 psi concrete, and soft sandstone is more like 1,000 psi concrete.

Once a bolt has been installed, it's impossible to see what's going on beneath the surface (like with the length of the bolt), and all that can be seen is the head of the bolt, again making identification of the type of bolt more difficult.

For more in-depth information, peruse "mechanical anchors" on the Powers company

Protection and Anchoring **139**

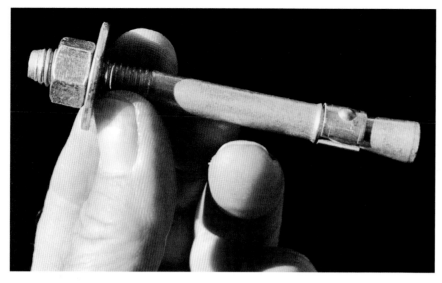

⅜-inch threaded expansion bolt.

website (www.powers.com); there is an excellent tutorial on the various types of bolts and how strong they are in differing rock types.

Even if lacking expertise in mechanical engineering or in identifying bolt design and type, it is important to know what to watch for when inspecting a bolt anchor. An obvious red flag is rust. SMC "death hangers," Leeper hangers, homemade aluminum hangers, and any bolt or hanger with obvious signs of corrosion should not be trusted. Look closely and identify the diameter of the bolt. A ⅜-inch diameter bolt has become the minimum

⅜-inch Powers expansion bolt with stainless steel Mad Rock hanger.

⅜-inch stainless steel Powers bolt with stainless steel Petzl hanger, painted to match the rock color.

Beware the ¼-inch Bolts

As someone who has replaced many bolts over the years, I (BG) can tell you that any ¼-inch bolt should be considered suspect, particularly in less than perfect rock. I've plucked out many ¼-inch contraction bolts that came out with about the same resistance as a nail being pulled out of plywood. To replace a ¼-inch bolt, the best method is to pry it out of its hole, then re-drill the same hole to a ½-inch diameter and install a ½-inch diameter stainless steel Powers Power Bolt (10,000 lbs. shear strength) with a stainless steel hanger. I like to paint the hanger (before I install it) the same color as the rock so that the bolt is visually unobtrusive. It's a good feeling to replace a ticking time bomb with a solid anchor that will last a lifetime.

A well-engineered rappel anchor. Both bolts are ⅜-inch stainless Powers bolts with stainless steel Petzl hangers, along with a stainless steel chain, quick link, and ring. Everything was painted before installation to match the color of the rock.

All these old bolts at Joshua Tree were replaced with brand-new stainless steel hardware, courtesy of the American Safe Climbing Association (ASCA).

standard, along with a stainless steel hanger. A bolt with threads and a nut holding the hanger in place is generally not as strong as the hex head types.

The rock should not show cracks emanating from the bolt placement—a more common problem with contraction bolts than expansion bolts.

In a good placement, the hanger should be flush against the rock and should not budge or be deformed in any way. A "spinner" is a bolt that protrudes enough so that the hanger can be easily spun around 360 degrees. This generally means that when the bolt was installed, the hole was not drilled

deeply enough, and the bolt contacted the bottom of the hole before the hanger could be drawn flush against the rock.

If the bolt wiggles slightly when pulled or the hanger is loose, and the bolt has a hex head or a nut on threads, tightening the bolt with a wrench may help, but most likely the bolt has a problem that can't be fixed. If, while trying to tighten it, no increasing resistance is felt, and it won't tighten any further, then the bolt has serious problems—usually this means the tolerance (diameter) of the hole is too big for the bolt, or the rock is too soft.

This rack has a good assortment of both nuts and camming devices.

The American Safe Climbing Association (ASCA) has been very active in donating the necessary (and expensive) hardware to climbers who take on the task of upgrading unsafe bolt anchors with modern, stainless steel bolts and hangers. To support their efforts and donate to the ASCA, visit www .safeclimbing.org.

CHAPTER 8

Anchor Systems

If the hundreds of pages of how-to literature, magazine articles, blogs, lengthy message board posts, and hours of instruction from professionals and climbing partners teach us nothing else, it's that anchors are something climbers pay attention to. And yet, much of what is said and has been said is facile. Most climbing anchors involve the simple combination of obvious components, using strong materials to make an unquestionably effective master point. As climbing instructors, and as climbers too, there is a tendency to obsess over the outliers, conflate simple problems and complex solutions, and worry ourselves. This section will attempt to differentiate between the simple tools used to solve simple problems that instructors are likely to encounter, and the more complex tools used to solve complicated problems that instructors will rarely encounter.

A simple three-point cordelette anchor.

For every anchor, simple or complex, the need for an unquestionably reliable, strong, and secure attachment point is the goal. The responsibility for managing risk of harm to others should inspire an anchor builder to create an anchor that can do the work of the climbing system, can easily sustain any potential loads that emergency scenarios may create, and can still give the entire climbing team a margin of error. So how strong is that? How strong would something have to be to eliminate all doubt?

Let us begin by considering the base-managed toprope, the system where the toprope has been redirected through the anchor and the climber and the belayer are on the ground. If the climber weighs 100 pounds, the belayer must match that weight in order to arrest the climber; therefore, we'll call the belayer a counterweight. At any point in a taut climbing system, the anchor must be able to hold the climber (100 lbs.) and the counterweight (100 lbs.); that's 200 pounds. But the climbing system is not always perfectly taut. The latent elongation of the climbing rope means that the climber is always a mass in motion, a mass on a sort of bungee cord when he or she falls. With a perfect belay, let's say that the climber's dynamic weight is more like 200 pounds. Now the counterweight is 200 pounds too, and the anchor must hold 400 pounds. Now let's say that the climber moves faster than the belayer can belay, or the belayer is a bit inattentive, and the falling climber now generates an even bigger dynamic load. Four hundred pounds is not inconceivable, and matched by a 400-pound counterweight, the anchor needs to hold 800 pounds. Now, if we could conceivably create an 800-pound load, how strong would the anchor need to be to create an unquestionably reliable, strong, secure attachment point? Now consider that climbing instructors are often taking all kinds of people climbing, people who weigh more than 100 pounds, for example. How strong would the anchor need to be? More than 800 pounds, surely. More than 2,000 pounds? More than 3,000? There is no definite

answer. "Unquestionably reliable, strong, and secure" might mean different things to all of us. That is both the challenge and the beauty of anchor building.

The goal of this chapter is to demonstrate skills that will allow an instructor to build an anchor that not only solves this problem effectively, but provides a reasonable margin of safety. Since all climbing gear, attachment tools, carabiners, protection, and ropes are overly strong, we should be able to build anchors that solve the problem unquestionably well.

Fundamental Anchor Anatomy and Principles

All anchors have the same fundamental anatomy. They have components, attachments, and a master point. Most anchors also have a shelf. Together these create the acronym, CAMS.

C = Components are the features or tools that ground an anchor to the landscape. They are often organized into natural (trees, boulders, terrain features) and artificial (bolts, pitons, removable protection) categories.

A = Attachments are the materials that combine the relative strength of each component and consolidate their strength in a focal point.

M = Master point is the point of the anchor where all critical attachments occur.

S = Shelf. Some anchors also have a shelf, an auxiliary attachment point with all the same load-bearing and security qualities as the master point. It should only be used in an auxiliary fashion.

All anchors should strive to adhere to the following fundamental principles:

1. Eliminate or limit extension: Given the failure of any individual part of the anchor, the attachment systems will not extend enough to severely shock load the remaining components.

2. Redundancy: Given the failure of any feature of the anchor system (with the exception of

a monolithic component), there will be other features to reinforce or back up that initial failure.

3. Intelligent load distribution: Given any load the anchor may sustain during its use, the attachment system should distribute load to the components in a manner that optimizes the relative strength and security of each component.

4. Strength: All attachments, components, knots, rock, or natural features must have more than adequate strength to sustain any load that could be applied to it during a climbing activity.

5. Simplicity: Given the anchoring tools available, the available components, and the prevailing conditions, an anchor should be efficiently constructed and deconstructed; while accomplishing all the other principles of anchoring, it should make efficient use of time and equipment.

Notes on Redundancy

By itself, redundancy does not guarantee safety—rappelling off a bunch of old weathered slings or a couple of old rusty chain links, for example—but redundancy in anchor systems is something to always strive for as a baseline and a starting point for evaluation. In rock climbing, a nonredundant anchor is considered marginal by professional standards. Many canyoneering enthusiasts argue that redundancy at the anchor system is superfluous, as there will be a point in the system where redundancy can no longer be maintained—rappelling on only one rope, with one rappel device, on one locking carabiner. This is absolutely true, so it's important to remember why redundancy is important to climbers. Unlike the canyoneering participant on rappel, or the military unit launching out of a helicopter, climbers are intentionally challenging themselves by climbing unknown

difficulties. There is nothing unpredictable about a rappel; the line will be loaded consistently and in the same direction. But a rock climber's movements are erratic and unpredictable, with wide variation from one climber to the next, especially on a challenging climb. Systemic redundancy is a way to create a satisfactory margin of error to account for that unpredictability. Sometimes instructors might intentionally modify the concept of redundancy if they can substitute supervision to provide the security that redundancy might otherwise offer. The rope direct belay is a good example. A thoughtful instructor knows that the principle of redundancy is not simply being ignored, but that redundancy is not necessarily the goal. Security is the goal; redundancy is just one of the most common ways to create that security.

The Rope Direct Belay

If the belay anchor is initially built well back from the edge, and you want to belay from the edge to maintain a visual on the climber who's climbing up from below, you can use the climbing rope and a rope direct belay technique, which is essentially belaying off an extended master point. Attach your climbing rope to the master point on the anchor with a clove hitch on a locking carabiner, so you can adjust the length and position yourself just where you'd like at a stance near the edge where you can see the climber. Off the back side of the clove hitch, leave a little slack, then tie a figure eight loop and clip it into a separate locking carabiner to the master point. On this strand of rope, tie a figure eight loop and clip in your assisted braking device (ABD), at an ergonomic position slightly above you (toward the anchor) but not so far away that you can't reach the device and manipulate the handle if need be. This method is referred to as "rope direct" because you are essentially belaying directly off the anchor, albeit extended whatever distance is required to position you at the edge. Using a device like a Grigri, you'll have the benefit of a quick and

The rope direct belay rigging. This rigging technique allows you to position yourself away from the anchor and still use the direct belay technique, albeit on an extended master point. The belayer is attached to the master point with a clove hitch to a locking carabiner. Off the back side of the clove hitch, the rope is clipped back to a separate carabiner with a figure eight loop. Off this strand, the Grigri is clipped to another figure eight loop. Here the distance is fairly close to the anchor, but this rigging technique is most useful for greater distances between the anchor and your desired belay stance, limited only by the length of available rope. The big advantage is visual contact with your climber in situations where the anchor is some distance back from the edge.

Students practice rigging a uniform load anchor system using double loop figure eights. The master point is tied with a BHK.

easy conversion to a raising system if required, and it's easy to lower someone on this setup by redirecting the brake strand on the Grigri.

Notes on Load Distribution

Most toproping situations involve an anchor that is uniformly loaded in a single direction. This is true of top-managed and base-managed climbs. Most anchor systems involve components that have comparable strength: a pair of bolts, a trio of cams in a similar size range, a combination of strong natural and removable components. In these cases, load distribution is fairly simple. A cordelette and 48-inch slings allow an anchor builder to pull tension on the components and tie a strong overhand or figure eight knot to ensure that the load is theoretically distributed to all the components. But in this configuration these anchors have been proven to have misleading load distributions. They do not in fact equalize the total load between the components. John Long argued this point compellingly in *Climbing Anchors*. John maintained that even if one could achieve equalization, the slightest shift in the direction of load would

Four-piece uniform load anchor pre-equalized with a cordelette in the anticipated direction of load. If the load shifts even slightly, all of the load will come to bear on a single piece. If that piece were to fail, the vector would shift to the next piece to load, albeit with minimal extension from the cordelette. The cordelette system is essentially a series of backups rigged with minimal extension.

This toprope anchor, rigged using the Joshua Tree System, is an example of a variable load (aka self-equalizing) anchor system.

Each leg of the V is connected to two camming devices rigged with magic Xs and load-limiting knots on 48-inch nylon slings. If the direction of load shifts slightly, the magic Xs will adjust accordingly to distribute the load on each leg of the V.

distort that equalization. He further noted that even if the load was 100 percent uniform and equalization was 100 percent perfect, he would still suggest to the anchor builder that not all the components are of equal merit, deserving an equal share of the load. When necessary, a more effective anchor builder ignores the idea of equalization and intentionally manipulates the distribution of the total load. In the following examples we will describe simple, timely systems that are most appropriate when complex load distributions are not necessary, as well as more complex systems used to intelligently distribute load to components when the load varies in direction and the components are not equally strong.

The Cordelette: A simple solution to a common anchoring problem

The cordelette system is an attachment system where the anchor builder ties off the cordelette in the anticipated direction of load. If the direction of load shifts slightly in any direction, all the load goes onto one placement (albeit with minimal extension). For toprope anchor systems, in most cases it is simple to determine the direction the anchor system will be loaded in, so a simple solution like the cordelette makes sense most of the time. Using the cordelette in this manner, the anchor builder essentially creates a system of backups. If one piece fails, the load transfers instantly to the remaining pieces with minimal shock loading, since the rigging limits extension.

The cordelette can be used to attach two, three, four, or even five placements to a master point, so it is versatile as well as simple. For two placements, like a two-bolt anchor, start by doubling the cordelette, then clip the doubled strand into both bolts with a pair of carabiners. Pull down between the bolts in a manner that targets the anticipated load, gather all the strands together, and tie an overhand or figure eight on a bight. There should be four strands of cord at the master point.

To rig three or four placements, clip the cordelette into all the placements, pull down between the

Simple two-bolt anchor rigged with a Tech cord (5,000 pounds tensile strength) cordelette. The cordelette is doubled to start with, producing four strands at the master point loop, and the climbing rope is clipped into three oval carabiners opposed and reversed.

pieces in a manner that targets the anticipated load, gather all the loops together, and tie an overhand or figure eight on a bight. Many instructors like to clip a carabiner into all the gathered loops and pull in the anticipated loading direction, then tie a figure eight knot with the carabiner attached to help even out all the strands.

Demonstration of pre-equalized cordelette with three anchor placements, tied with a 7mm nylon cordelette. A clove hitch has been tied to the top left piece to keep the double fisherman's knot away from the end loops. This is a simple and effective rig as long as the direction of load is predetermined, which is most often the case when toproping.

This four-piece anchor is pre-equalized with a 7mm nylon cordelette. The overhand knot creates a four-loop master point to which the two opposed and reversed locking carabiners are clipped.

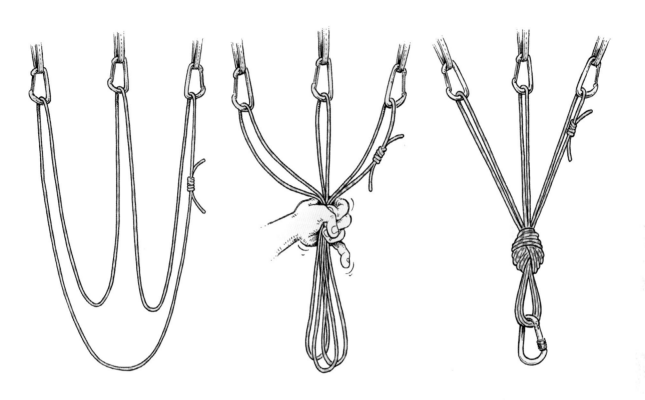

An 18- to 20-foot-long cordelette is usually long enough to equalize three or four anchor points, as long as they are not spaced too far apart. Use a sling or two if necessary to get all the carabiners you'll be clipping into within a workable range. Clip a single strand of the cordelette into each carabiner, then pull down between the pieces and gather the loops (with three pieces you'll have three loops). Clipping a carabiner into the loops before tying the knot will make it easier to equalize all the strands. Tie a figure eight knot to create your master point, which should be roughly 3 to 4 inches in diameter. If you don't have enough cord to tie a figure eight, an overhand knot takes up less cord.

The drawback of the cordelette system (left) is that if the direction of the anticipated load changes, one piece in the anchor takes all the load (right). Think of the cordelette system as a system of backups: If the one piece that is loaded fails, the load goes onto the next piece with relatively minimal extension in the system. For toproping anchors, since the load on the anchor system is relatively low, the cordelette system has the advantage of being easy to use and simple to rig, negating any potential for shock loading.

The Sliding X

The sliding X (aka magic X) is a simple way to distribute load to two anchor points with a sling, creating an anchor system that adjusts as the load shifts in one direction or another. If using the sliding X with a long sling (like a sewn, 48-inch double-length sling), it is possible to minimize extension by tying overhand knots just above the clip-in point. This allows the system to adjust, but limits any extension if one piece fails. Or two single-length slings can be used together with a sliding X, creating a redundant rig with minimal extension.

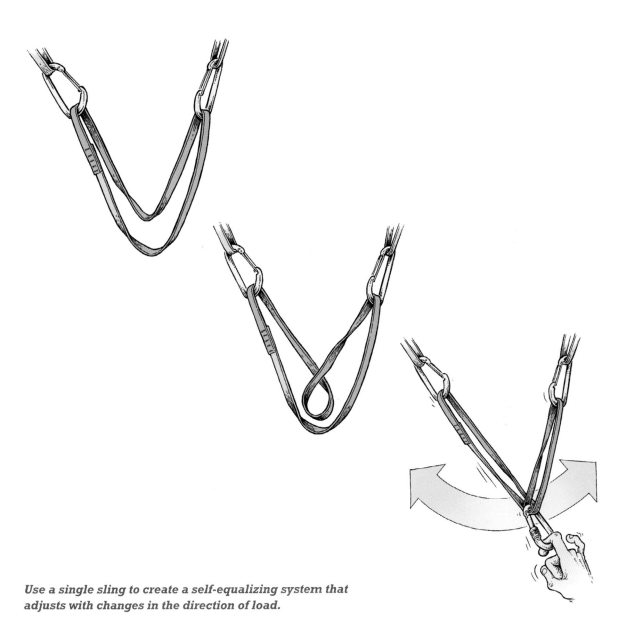

Use a single sling to create a self-equalizing system that adjusts with changes in the direction of load.

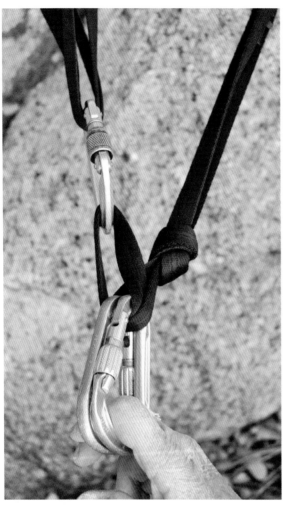 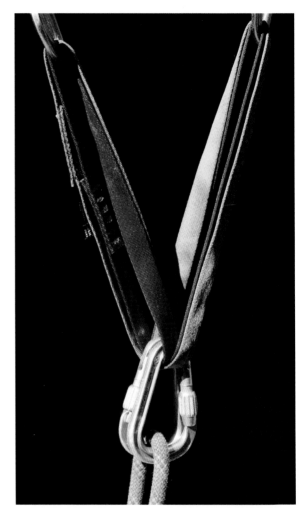

As an anchor system, this rigging is not redundant. For the sling itself to be redundant, there must be an overhand knot tied on both sides of the sliding X.

A simple two-bolt anchor can be rigged with a sliding X using two slings and two locking carabiners at the master point for a redundant, self-equalizing system. With a two-bolt anchor, many instructors use locking carabiners on the bolt hangers too. The drawback of this rig is that if one bolt were to fail, the system would extend to the length of the slings. As a general rule of thumb, limit the maximum extension in your anchor system to half the length of a single (24-inch) sling.

The Quad

The quad is a slightly more complicated system for a variable load direction using a cordelette. It's a great system to use for toprope anchors. It gives near perfect equalization with minimal extension and great strength. To rig the quad, start by doubling a cordelette, then grab the middle with the fist. Tie an overhand knot on each side of the fist, and it is ready to rig. Clip the double-strand loops into the bolts with locking carabiners, then clip only three of the four strands at the master point, leaving one loop outside the master point carabiners. This ensures that if one bolt fails, carabiners remain clipped into a pocket on the master point.

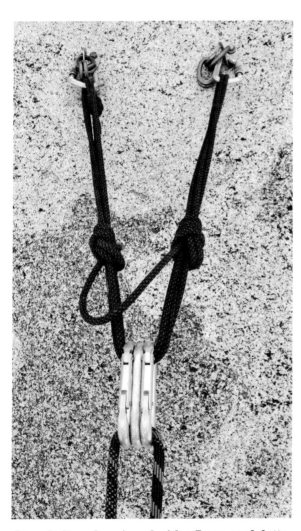

A two-bolt anchor rigged with a 7mm cordelette and the quad system.

The cordelette is clipped directly to the bolt hangers with locking carabiners, bypassing the cheap hardware store lap links (which are only rated at around 1,000 lbs.).

Detail of quad rig master point with three ovals opposed and reversed.

Detail of quad rig with two locking carabiners opposed and reversed.

Stacked Sliding Xs

This gives you a complex rig for a variable load with slings. Occasionally an anchor builder encounters anchor configurations that have components with very different strengths. Imagine a narrow 4-inch crack that immediately closes to a ½-inch crack running along the top of the crag. An effective anchor builder understands that a 4-inch SLCD is much stronger and has a much higher margin of error in its placement (due to its large camming range). By comparison, ½-inch SLCDs are weaker and have a minuscule camming range. These components are not equally strong, and therefore distributing load to them in an equal manner would not take advantage of their relative strengths and weaknesses. In other words, equalizing the pieces would not be an intelligent distribution of the load. An effective alternative would be to build a sliding

Here the green sling equalizes two components of lesser strength than the top right piece. Although this anchor system achieves good equalization and logical load distribution, it is not redundant because the red sling is not redundant at the master point.

The rigging is now made redundant by tying an extension-limiting overhand knot on each side of the sliding X, although the green sling will not minimize extension.

Here the rigging is redundant with minimal extension. The two pieces on the left have been equalized with the red 48-inch nylon sling, using a sliding X and extension-limiting overhand knots. The yellow 48-inch nylon sling equalizes this point to the single, strongest piece in the anchor, again with a sliding X and extension-limiting overhand knots.

X with load-limiting knots between the two ½-inch SLCDs, creating a mini–master point. Then a second sliding X with load-limiting knots would connect the 4-inch SLCD to the first sliding X, to that mini–master point.

The Equalette

The equalette is a complex rig for a variable load direction using a cordelette. It gives the anchor builder four strands, or "legs," running from the master point to the various pieces in the anchor

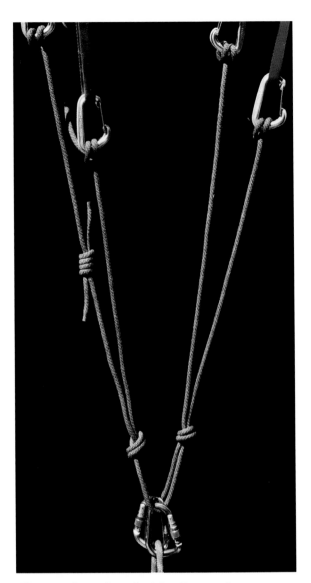

The equalette rigged with a 7mm nylon cordelette. This is a versatile system to use for equalizing three or four placements, giving you redundancy, equalization, and no extension. The only drawback is in its complexity and the fact that it does not have one singular master point to clip into. Here the equalette is rigged to four placements, using the various "arms" of the cordelette attached with clove hitches for easy adjustment.

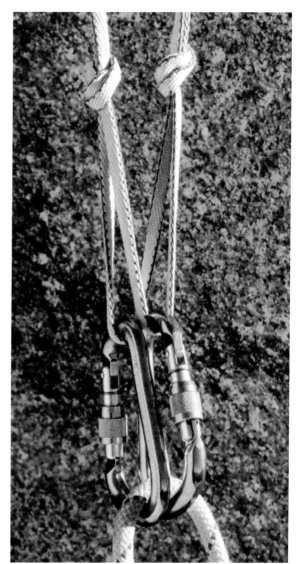

Detail of the equalette master point using two locking carabiners opposed and reversed.

Detail of equalette master point rigged with a Dyneema sling. Tying an overhand knot in a Dyneema sling reduces its strength by 50 percent; it's better to use a 7mm nylon cordelette when rigging the equalette, as you'll be tying lots of knots.

Detail of an equalette toproping rig tied with a doubled cordelette for a two-bolt anchor.

matrix. These four legs can be tied to the pieces with figure eights, clove hitches, or double loop knots like the double loop eight or double loop bowline.

To tie an equalette rig, form a U shape with the cordelette and grab the bottom of the U, positioning the fisherman's knot on the cordelette about 18 inches away from the bottom of the U. Tie an overhand knot on both sides of your fist, about 10 inches apart.

At the master point there will be two separate loops. Clip into each loop with a separate locking carabiner.

Vectors

A vector is a quantity that incorporates both direction and magnitude. Picture a tightrope walker balancing out on the middle of a wire. If he weighs 200 pounds, the load at each end where the wire is attached will be roughly 1,000 pounds. Why is this? When two anchor points are equalized, as the angle of the wire, sling, cord, or rope approaches 180 degrees, the forces at the anchor points increase drastically. When the angle is narrow, the load is distributed at around 50 percent to each anchor.

Keep this in mind when building toprope anchor systems. If the angle between two anchor points reaches 120 degrees, the load at each anchor is 100 percent. Strive to keep all the angles under 60 degrees to split the load roughly 50/50. A good way to help guarantee an intelligent load distribution is to keep the angles in an attachment system under 90 degrees. Also, avoid rigging a sling between two anchors in a triangular configuration (called the American Triangle), which, even at 90 degrees, places 1.3 times the force at each anchor point. An American Triangle rigged at 120 degrees would almost double the load at each anchor point!

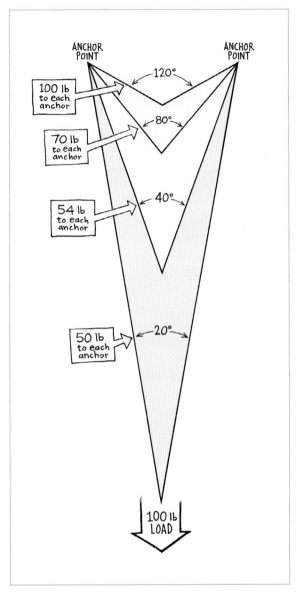

ANCHOR POINT   ANCHOR POINT

120°

100 lb to each anchor

80°

70 lb to each anchor

40°

54 lb to each anchor

20°

50 lb to each anchor

100 lb LOAD

This diagram illustrates how a 100-pound load is distributed between two anchor points at various angles. Keep the angle between two anchors as narrow as possible, striving to keep it under 60 degrees. At 120 degrees the load is 100 percent at each anchor! Think of 0 to 60 degrees as ideal, 60 to 90 degrees a caution zone, and over 90 degrees a danger zone.

American Triangle

Load per anchor with 100 lbs. of force

Bottom Angle	V Rigging	Triangle Rigging
30 degrees	52 lbs.	82 lbs.
60 degrees	58 lbs.	100 lbs.
90 degrees	71 lbs.	131 lbs.
120 degrees	100 lbs.	193 lbs.
150 degrees	193 lbs.	380 lbs.

The American Triangle rigged at a rappel anchor. Avoid rigging with a triangle configuration—it adds unnecessary forces to your anchor points. Stick to a V configuration for lower loads.

CHAPTER 9

Advanced Anchor Rigging Systems and Institutional Anchors

In the previous chapter, fundamental anchoring principles were discussed with strategies to create an unquestionably effective attachment point. Those principles will carry an anchor builder through all disciplines in climbing. The Single Pitch Instructor, however, will also require further skills for establishing an anchor and setting a toprope, because there are a few challenges that are unique to a Single Pitch Instructor's terrain:

1. Sometimes the components in an anchor, natural or otherwise, are far apart from each other, too far for a cordelette or a 48-inch sling.

2. The cliff's edge is an especially dangerous place for an instructor who is trying to keep safe and supervise participants.

3. When working at the base of a climb, a master point of the anchor has to be positioned in a place that is hazardous, such as over the cliff's edge.

Using a Setup Rope: Components Far Apart

Thankfully, a Single Pitch Instructor can bring along extra tools for anchor building. Unlike a multi-pitch or alpine climbing team, a single pitch team can afford to carry a little bit of extra weight. A length of static or low-stretch rope is worth every ounce of extra weight. To use it effectively and efficiently, an instructor should be able to stand at the site of the intended master point, look back into the terrain, select potential components, then use the setup rope to connect those components to the master point. A common sequence might proceed as follows:

1. Determine the climb and a distance from the cliff's edge directly above the climb where there is little risk of falling over the edge.

2. Face the terrain and use raised arms to target potential components (trees, boulders, removable and permanent protection). Let the arms forecast the vectors the setup rope will eventually create to make sure component selections are not too far apart.

3. Flake out the rope and take the end of the rope out to the most distant component. Attach the rope to that component in whatever manner is most efficient and effective.

4. Leave enough slack at the site of the intended master point to tie a BHK, then take the remaining bight of rope back to the other component.

5. Once both components are connected, a closed U shape awaits the anchor builder at the site of the intended master point. Use this bight of rope to tie a BHK that distributes load to the components along the anticipated direction of pull (toward the climb).

This sequence of connecting a setup rope to components and tying a BHK has limitless variations. Becoming efficient takes practice.

Instructor Tether: Managing Risk at the Cliff's Edge

Most climbers and climbing instructors alike have become familiar enough with the danger of the cliff's edge that their balance, their attentiveness, and their caution allow them to monitor and regulate proximity to a drop-off. Climbing instructors, however, cannot rely entirely on these skills because they are also supervising their students, observing the environment, and trying to complete setups efficiently. In other words, they are more distracted,

A simple tether using a cordelette. The instructor has girth-hitched the 7mm nylon cordelette through both tie-in points on the harness (then clipped to an anchor with a locking carabiner.

Here the cordelette has been threaded through both tie-in attachment points and tied with an overhand knot for redundancy to create a simple tether.

A simple tether using the rope tied with a clove hitch at the anchor.

and distraction is very dangerous indeed. Fortunately, climbing instructors have many options to secure themselves when in proximity to a cliff's edge; they can construct some form of instructor tether.

- Fixing a section of rope to an anchor allows an instructor many tethering options—using a Grigri, an ATC with friction hitch backup, a clove hitch, a full-strength sling with a klemheist, or even tying in to the rope.

- Any number of slings and cordelettes might work nicely to create a long leash. Instructors can girth-hitch one end of a closed loop to the harness and attach the opposite end of the loop to the master point.

- The climbing rope itself is always an obvious tethering tool. Instructors can easily tie in with a figure eight follow-through and then attach the climbing rope to the anchor with a clove hitch.

When using a Grigri on an instructor tether, tie an overhand knot backup whenever you take your brake hand off the rope. Always tie a stopper knot in the end of a rope tether to close the system.

Extensions: Creating a Master Point Over the Cliff's Edge

Once an instructor has a master point and a tethering method, it may be necessary to create an extension for a secondary master point, which will allow a base-managed toprope to run through a pair of carabiners free and clear of the cliff's edge. Many instructors refer to this secondary master point as the action point, or hot point. Either way, since it is a part of the anchor, the same fundamental principles that govern the master point should also govern the extension. For a typical extension, the instructor might attach a section of static or low-stretch rope to the initial master point with an overhand or figure eight loop then feed out a loop of slack that hangs over the cliff's edge, closing the long loop with another overhand or figure eight loop. Now, using the tether, an instructor can comfortably and securely set up a position at or just over the edge to tie a BHK. This is the point where the climbing rope will finally be placed.

Systems Using a Setup Rope

Aside from being the best tool for the individual tasks mentioned so far, a setup rope further proves itself as an elegant and efficient anchoring tool because it can be used to accomplish all three tasks—combine components, build tethers, and create extensions. When the full range of possibilities are understood by a climbing instructor, certain patterns emerge in the use of the tool; we call those patterns "systems." It should be understood, however, that the most elegant and efficient use of the tool often involves a combination of the techniques demonstrated. An instructor will want to explore the most applicable terrain, the programmatic options, and the economy of materials used for each technique when deciding how to use the setup rope to build a given anchor.

The Joshua Tree System— V Rigging with Extension Rope

Most anchors in Joshua Tree National Park in California require gear placements set well back from the cliff's edge, and bolted anchors are a rarity. Out of necessity, instructors at Joshua Tree developed a system to rig toprope anchors that is both efficient and redundant, using a length of low-stretch rope.

To rig the Joshua Tree System, visualize a V configuration, with two separate sets of anchors on the top of the V, and the point, or bottom, of the V being the toprope master point over the edge of the cliff. Ideally, the angle of the V should be as narrow as possible—at least less than 90 degrees. Once you have determined where the climb is and where you want your master point, picture the V in your mind and begin to set your anchors. If using natural anchors, it could be as simple as two trees. For simplicity let's say we have two anchors: anchor A and anchor B. Start by attaching one end of your static rigging rope to anchor A. This can be done either by using a sling or cordelette and a locking carabiner to a figure eight loop, or by tying the rope directly around the tree. (The re-threaded bowline works well for tying a rope to a tree.)

Now, to increase security as you approach the cliff's edge, protect yourself by taking a 48-inch nylon sling and attaching it to your rigging rope with a klemheist knot. The 48-inch sling with klemheist is an excellent full-strength tether option in this system; be sure to attach the sling to the belay loop with a locking carabiner. A nylon sling is better for this application because nylon has some stretch, whereas Spectra or Dyneema are static (like a wire cable) and have no stretch. Now you can slide the klemheist knot up and down the rigging rope to safeguard yourself as you work near the edge. Tie a BHK so that your master point dangles just over the lip of the cliff's edge, positioned directly above your chosen climb. Attach your climbing rope with carabiners (either two opposed and reversed locking, or three opposed and reversed ovals) and run the rope back to anchor B, attaching it with a clove hitch to a locking carabiner. This will allow you to adjust the tension and fine-tune the load distribution.

The Joshua Tree System allows the anchor builder to tether to a leg of the anchoring system. That's why the klemheist and 48-inch nylon sling is an important selection for tethering—any other method would not allow the anchor builder to precisely position the master point. But it is almost exclusively a system used for base-site climbing anchors, since neither of the component anchors are positioned directly above the climb and the master point itself is positioned so far below the edge of the climb that top-site management would be impractical. The Joshua Tree System also boasts excellent material economy. It only requires enough material to extend out to the cliff's edge; that is, two times the distance between the component anchors and the edge (with a little extra for knot tying).

Personal Preference

I (BG) prefer to tie both legs of the V into anchor points using figure eight loops. I know from experience that the BHK takes about 4 feet of rope to tie. So I'll tie both ends of the V first, with about 4 feet of the extension rope dangling over the edge, weighted down by a few carabiners to find my equalization point. Then I'll pull the point of the V back up and tie my BHK last.

Proper use of a friction hitch for security while rigging a toprope. Here the instructor is tethered with a 48-inch nylon sling, attached to one leg of the setup rope with a klemheist knot and clipped into the harness belay loop with a locking carabiner.

Overview of the Joshua Tree System. The right "leg" of the extension rope is attached with a figure eight loop to a locking carabiner clipped to a master point on a three-piece anchor pre-equalized with a cordelette. The left leg of the extension rope goes to a two-piece anchor pre-equalized with another cordelette, attached with a clove hitch on a locking carabiner for adjustment of the extension rope. A BHK is tied for the master point, with two opposed and reversed locking carabiners ready for the climbing rope.

Close-up of the master point on the Joshua Tree System using a BHK and three steel oval carabiners with the gates opposed and reversed.

Toprope all day long with your extension rope rubbing on a sharp edge . . .

. . . and you'll end up with a seriously abraded rope like this one.

A commercially made edge protector, like this one sold by Petzl, is a wise investment. Attach it to the rigging rope with a friction hitch.

This finished rig illustrates the simplicity of the Joshua Tree System, with the lower leg connected to two anchors using a double loop figure eight. The upper leg was connected last, using a clove hitch to a locking carabiner for equalization, attached to two pieces and a doubled sling. Note the edge protector guarding both legs of the extension rope from abrasion.

Take care to make sure the extension rope is not resting over sharp edges at the lip of the cliff. This setup is an "unmonitored" anchor system, which means that once rigged, the climbing instructor will be at the base and not able to watch what is happening at the anchor—like the extension rope abrading over an edge, so take special care to prevent this by padding the edge; a pack or rope bag will work or, better yet, use commercially made edge protectors.

If you learn to tie double loop knots like the double loop figure eight and double loop bowline, along with the in-line figure eight, you'll be able to eliminate many slings and cordelettes from your anchor system and become more efficient in your rigging.

The Lifeline System—
V Rigging with Instructor Tether

This is a variation of the Joshua Tree rigging method. Instead of tethering with a klemheist and a 48-inch sling, an instructor may find it advantageous to tether with a fixed section of rope. While the Joshua Tree System attaches the end of the rope to one of the component anchors, the Lifeline System attaches a figure eight with a bight so that two load-bearing strands are available for use. The one strand is only long enough

Example of V rigging with a tether. Each leg of the V consists of two bomber pieces. The bottom leg is equalized to the two placements with a double loop bowline, and the top leg (with tether) is equalized with a double loop figure eight.

to access the cliff's edge and serves as an instructor tether, while the second becomes the same leg of the anchor system that the Joshua Tree System utilizes. The important concept to remember here is that the tether should be clipped into a bona fide, redundant anchor—not just a single piece of gear.

An astute instructor should immediately conclude that this variation of the Joshua Tree System does not have the same material economy as its forbearer. While the Joshua Tree System only requires two lengths of material to connect the component anchors to the master point, the Lifeline will

Here the instructor has rappelled using an instructor tether to approach the edge in low-angle but exposed terrain to make some adjustments on his BHK master point toprope rig. Whenever you take your brake hand off the Grigri in low-angle terrain, tie a backup knot (overhand loop) as shown here, because if you unweight the Grigri, the rope can slide through. Always tie a stopper knot on the end of your tether before you begin using it.

require three, with a little extra for knot tying, of course.

Instructors may find the Lifeline to be an effective system if the other half of the anchor, the second component anchor, is in a precarious or inaccessible place. The Lifeline would provide access to those components so that the anchor can be completed. The Lifeline is also an excellent tool for probing an ambiguous cliff's edge to pinpoint the location of the climb. Lastly, the Lifeline might be an excellent tool to access anchoring hardware normally intended for sport climbing use. Such anchors are typically installed over the cliff's edge, where access from above may not only be atypical, but dangerous without the Lifeline System.

The Backside System— Pre-Equalized Extensions

Unlike the Joshua Tree or Lifeline Systems, the Backside System preestablishes a space for both a top-managed system and a bottom-managed system at the same time. In the simplest terms, this is done by setting up a V configuration and tying two BHKs into it. The top BHK becomes the master point for top management. The backside of that top BHK should be long enough to droop over the edge of the cliff, where a second BHK is tied. The bottom BHK then becomes the master point for bottom-managed operations.

Similar to the Joshua Tree System, an instructor will be tethered to a leg of the anchor system. A 48-inch nylon sling tied as a klemheist is a logical choice for tethering.

The Backside System can boast certain material economies that the Joshua Tree and Lifeline Systems cannot because it does require entire component anchor points. It presumes that the initial master point will be positioned above the climb. But its greatest strength is its programmatic versatility. As mentioned, it can easily be used for top-managed sites as well as base-managed sites. Furthermore, when built in anticipation of both kinds of activities,

it allows the instructor to quickly transition from one to the other.

Rigging the Backside System

1. Configure a Joshua Tree V with a loop of rope hanging over the edge of the cliff. Make sure to estimate for the amount of rope that will be eaten up by the dual BHKs.

2. Determine where you would like your top-managed high master point to be and tie a BHK there. The backside of the BHK should be long enough to hang over the edge of the cliff.

3. Tie a second BHK in the loop that hangs over the edge. There are two options to secure the toprope BHK: Pass the BHK through the backside of the knot or clip all three loops of the BHK into the toprope carabiners.

4. Use a klemheist with a 48-inch nylon sling to tether to one of the ropes directly below the high master point. Do not clip into this friction hitch until you are ready to make a transition to the bottom.

5. If operating from the high master point, pull the backside of the high master point up and stack it out of the way.

Making the Transition from Rigging to Rappelling

When using any of the aforementioned systems, if you decide to rappel to the base, you will need to transition from some tethering tool to rappelling. In all three systems, it is reasonable to tether over the cliff's edge to access the climbing rope. Fixed sections of rope with ABDs make this transition quite easy, because the instructor can rappel over the edge instead of downclimbing while adjusting a klemheist. Once in position over the cliff's edge, pull up your doubled rappel rope, rig your rappel device, and back it up with an autoblock. Once the rappel is correctly rigged and double-checked, the original tethering system may be deconstructed.

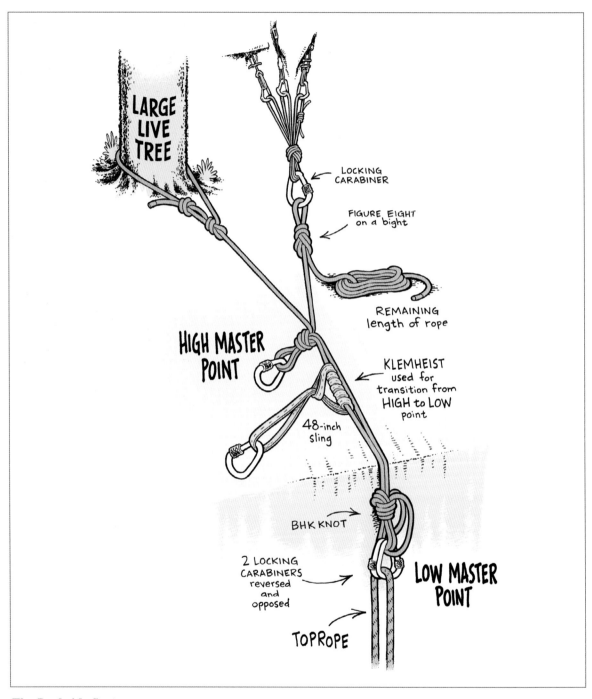

The Backside System.

MIKE CLELLAND

AMGA Single Pitch Instructor Richard Riquelme managing a climber on a Backside System. Note that the pre-equalized strands are uphill and out of the way.

JASON D. MARTIN

Loading the Backside of a BHK

I t may strike an instructor as unusual to load the backside of a BHK in this manner. Although this application does not conform to the way instructors have typically seen a BHK in use, it is an acceptable way to load a BHK. It is essentially a double flat overhand. As long as the resultant BHK loop is either in use or adequately long enough, it is highly unlikely that a climbing team could create a load large enough to compromise the backside use of the BHK.

Making the transition on an instructor tether with an ABD. The instructor pre-rigged his rappel device—extended on a doubled nylon sling and backed up with an autoblock knot attached with a locking carabiner to his belay loop. Once he descends on the tether below the master point and weights his pre-rigged system, he can double-check everything before unclipping the Grigri.

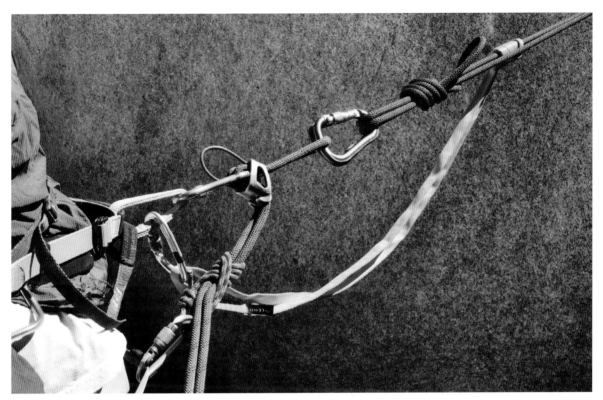

Making a transition with a 48-inch sling attached to one strand of the rigging rope with a klemheist knot. The rappel device is backed up with an autoblock. This technique could be used to transition to a rappel using the Backside or Joshua Tree Systems.

The Three-in-One System

Popularized by Adam Fox during his tenure as the AMGA's SPI Discipline Coordinator, the Three-in-One System was conceived as an efficient rigging system for professional instructors that addresses the needs for instructor security, top-managed scenarios, and easy conversion to a bottom-managed site. Instructors around the country have learned to appreciate its signature elegance, since it manages to anchor, create an instructor tether, and create an extension with the same rope. Three tasks with one rope: Three-in-One.

Even in its simplest configuration, the Three-in-One System will require enough rope to accomplish all these tasks. An instructor can anticipate the amount of rope needed by multiplying the distance between the components and the cliff's edge by three. If the components are farther from the cliff's edge than a third of the setup rope length, the Three-in-One System may not be effective.

Start by building a high master point in much the same sequence as previously discussed:

1. Locate the climb and a distance from the cliff's edge directly above the climb that reduces the risk of falling over the edge.

2. Face the terrain and use raised arms to target potential components (trees, boulders, removable and permanent protection). Let the

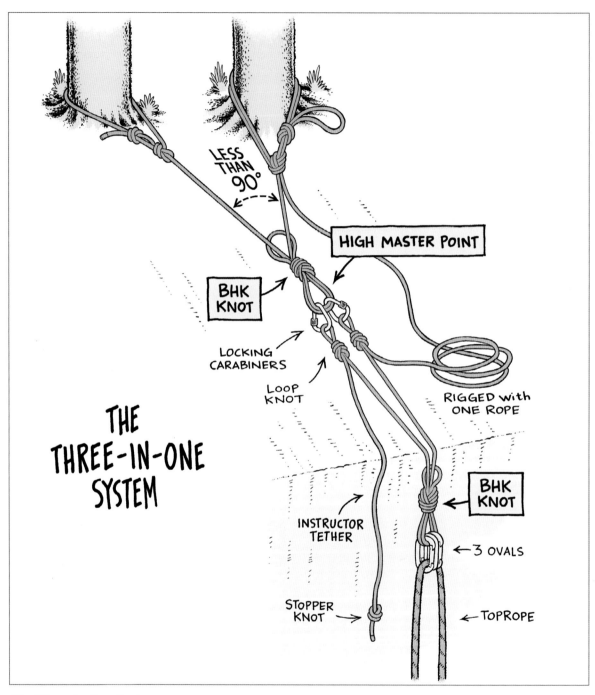

LESS THAN 90°

HIGH MASTER POINT

BHK KNOT

LOCKING CARABINERS

LOOP KNOT

RIGGED with ONE ROPE

THE THREE-IN-ONE SYSTEM

INSTRUCTOR TETHER

BHK KNOT

3 OVALS

STOPPER KNOT

TOPROPE

The Three-in-One System.

MIKE CLELLAND

arms forecast the vectors the setup rope will eventually create to make sure the component selections are not too far apart. Keep in mind that a narrow-angle V configuration (or at least less than 90 degrees) is the goal.

3. Flake out the rope and take the end of the rope out to the most distant component. Strive to use the setup rope alone to attach the component. Bowlines can be very helpful.

4. Leave enough slack at the site of the intended master point to tie a BHK, then take the remaining bight of rope back to the other component. Again, try to attach the bight directly to the component to avoid using some other tool; a bowline with a bight works well for this application.

5. Once both components are connected, a closed U shape awaits the anchor builder at the site of the intended master point. Use this bight of rope to tie a BHK that distributes the load to the components along the anticipated direction of pull (toward the climb).

Anchor Redundancy

In both of the illustrations included in this chapter, the rigging rope is tied off to two different bombproof anchor points. This is not a requirement. The rigging rope could go to two different anchor points, or it could go to a single solid anchor. For example, if you have a giant tree or a solid multi-piece traditional anchor, there is no need to build a second anchor. Both strands of the rigging rope could be attached to the same master point.

Now that the master point is built, use what is left of the setup rope to construct the rest of the system. Start with the instructor tether:

1. Since one end of the setup rope is tied to the most distant component, take the other end and tie a stopper knot.

2. Toss the stopper-knotted tail of rope so it hangs down about 10 feet below the cliff's edge.

3. With this distance measured, affix the rope to the master point using a figure eight loop and a locking carabiner.

4. With the attachment of a Grigri or assisted braking device, this fixed length of rope will be the instructor tether.

Next, an extension can easily be created using the rope that remains.

1. From the backside of the instructor tether, feed out a loop of slack that hangs over the cliff's edge.

2. Close the long loop with another overhand or figure eight loop.

3. Now, using the tether, an instructor can comfortably and securely position themselves at or just over the edge to tie a BHK.

Stepping back, an instructor should see that the entire system—anchor, tether, and extension—has been tied with the same setup rope.

Making the Transition from Rigging to Rappelling

To rappel back to the base, use the instructor tether to facilitate a secure, easy transition to a pre-rigged rappel. Simply pull up the doubled rappel rope, rig a rappel device, back it up with an autoblock, then rappel on the instructor tether with a Grigri until the rappel is tight to the pre-rigged rappel setup. Double-check the rappel device and make sure the autoblock is grabbing, then finally unclip from the Grigri and proceed with the rappel.

CHAPTER 10

Risk Management
at the Crag

Every year the American Alpine Club publishes *Accidents in North American Mountaineering,* detailing significant climbing accidents for the year in a comprehensive analysis. Studying what happened to other climbers can heighten an instructor's awareness of what to watch out for to avoid a mishap. John Dill, head of Yosemite's Search and Rescue (SAR) team, studied the most serious climbing accidents that happened in Yosemite Valley from 1970 to 1990. During that time fifty-one climbers died in accidents, 80 percent of them, Dill estimates, "easily preventable." In his article "Staying Alive," Dill points out that state of mind is the key to effective risk management: "It's impossible to know how many climbers were killed by haste or overconfidence, but many survivors will tell you that they somehow lost their good judgment long enough to get hurt. It's a complex subject and

Sign at Mountain Warfare Training Center, Leavitt Meadows, California.

Inattentional Blindness

*I*nattentional blindness is a term psychologists use to describe the neurological phenomenon that occurs when the brain fails to see something obvious, when attention is distracted or focused on something else. Psychologists who study multitasking have found that most of us aren't the multi-taskers we think we are: Our brain is simply switching back and forth from one activity to another, deactivating one area of focus to process the other task. In my (BG) role as an examiner for guides' certification exams, I've seen examples of inattentional blindness many times during complicated technical scenarios, where the instructor has moved his focus without seeing an obvious error, like a carabiner unlocked at a key belay or rappel device. It's as if the mind skipped a step, or the brain said that everything was correct and complete, when in fact it wasn't—a cognitive blind spot.

Psychologists theorize that once the brain determines what is important, it fills in the picture with whatever your expectations believe should be there. These failures of awareness happen to all of us, at one time or another, but we're not aware of them, so we don't realize what we've missed! A systematic and routine checklist is helpful, but what we really need to learn to look for is what might be wrong, not what looks right.

Pat Ament, the great Colorado climber of the 1960s and 1970s, writes in his book *Rock Wise:* "As with all of climbing, it is attitude that saves or kills. There is no better beginning than within the mind, in the form of complete concentration. There is no room for oversight or for dismissing what is logi-cally understood. Keen intuition must evaluate all which strikes both mind and eye. Preparing . . . is a process of reasoning and advancing through a regular chain of tests until a synthesis reads go."

sometimes a touchy one. Nevertheless . . . at least three states of mind frequently contribute to acci-dents: ignorance, casualness, and distraction."

Proper risk management in the single pitch environment involves identifying and assessing haz-ards, making the right decisions to avoid these haz-ards, then implementing controls and supervision to minimize the risks.

Rockfall

One environmental hazard is rockfall, which can be naturally occurring (caused by melting ice, wind, etc.) or more likely man-made, caused either by someone pulling off or stepping on a loose hold, or in most cases by a rope being pulled or dragged across the top edge or the face of the cliff. Dropped equipment is also a hazard. Setting up a helmet perimeter zone at the base of the cliff minimizes the danger, as does requiring students to not hang out at the very base of the cliff in the rockfall zone unless they are belaying or climbing. An explana-tion of the risk is appropriate (i.e., why you need to wear your helmet at the base and while belaying and climbing), as is an explanation of the universal verbal signal for a falling rock or dropped piece of equipment: "ROCK!" Being vigilant is the best strategy, especially when other climbers are directly above or at the top of the cliff.

Terrain Hazards

Another environmental hazard is the terrain itself. If working at the top of the cliff, falling off the edge is a real hazard, as is any steep and exposed terrain involved in scrambling up to the top. In very exposed situations a fixed line can be rigged. See chapter 14, Fixed Lines, for more information.

The base of the cliff also has terrain hazards. The ideal base for group classes would be perfectly flat, but this is often not the case or even possible. Showing students the proper approaches to the climb and belay spots and supervising them is important. Often the most dangerous aspect of taking a large group climbing in a toprope crag setting is their scrambling around on uneven terrain at the base of the cliff, unroped, where they aren't protected by a toprope. The use of ground anchors is important for the belayers in situations where there are chasms and drop-offs adjacent to the belay stances.

Closing the System

In the single pitch environment, the rope system should always be closed. This simple protocol will prevent many accidents during lowering and rappelling. A closed system means that both ends of the rope have a knot in them—either the end is tied into someone's harness, or a stopper knot is tied on a free end. This simple habit prevents the end of the rope from ever going through a belay or rappel device. Always close the system.

Systems Checks

The instructor is responsible for risk management for the entire group. A protocol for systematically checking every climber and belayer before every climb should be standard procedure. A commonly used system is to start with ABC: Check the ground anchor (if used), check the belayer, then check the climber. A proper systems check should be both

visual and verbal. The instructor should be close enough to clearly see the harness buckle and rope tie-in. A verbal check is important because it lets the student recognize and learn what to check for. The best method is to have the students themselves go through the checks, with instructor supervision, to get into the habit of a mandatory systems check before every climb.

Anchor

Check the ground anchor to make sure the belayer is in a line between the direction she will be pulled in the event of a fall and the anchor itself. A good way to attach the belayer to the ground anchor is with a clove hitch to a locking carabiner (the end is tied to the front of the belayer's harness with the standard figure eight follow-through knot).

Belayer

Check the belayer's harness, to make sure it is buckled properly. Check the figure eight follow-through knot, to make sure that it is (1) tied properly and (2) threaded through the correct tie-in points at the front of the harness. Check the belayer's belay device, to make sure the rope is properly threaded through the device, and lastly, check the belayer's locking carabiner on the belay device, to make sure that it is locked. Check that the belayer is wearing her helmet.

Climber

Check the climber's harness, to make sure it is buckled properly. Check the climber's figure eight follow-through knot, to make sure that it is (1) tied properly and (2) threaded through the correct tie-in points at the front of the harness. Check to ensure the climber is wearing his helmet.

These checks are simple, but it is surprising how many times students are caught making a mistake somewhere along these lines. The instructor needs to do these checks before every climb. It's that simple. Go through the checks with the students until they learn what to look for, and have the belayer/

climber pair go through the checks themselves with instructor supervision.

New instructors might want to come up with an acronym to help remember what to look for, such as CRASH:

C = carabiner (squeeze check the locking carabiners)

R = rope (check to make sure the rope is not twisted at the top anchor, and check the knots)

A = attitude (check to make sure the climber is ready or has any questions)

S = stuff (check for any extraneous stuff on the climber that should be removed)

H = helmet and harness

Another common one is BARCK:

B = buckles on the harness

A = anchor (check the ground anchor)

R = rope

C = carabiners locked

K = knots

Whatever system is used, know what to check for, and be methodical.

Falling

With a sound toprope anchor, a good belayer, a proper tie-in, and good systems check, the biggest risks the climber faces during the climb are from falling. If the belayer is attentive and there is minimal slack in the system, the fall will be short and uneventful. For novices a demo on how to fall is important, showing them the proper position if a fall does occur: a wide stance with the legs, leaning back to weight the harness, not grabbing onto the rope, extending both arms outward against the rock, not clutching the rock or grabbing handholds.

The falls to guard against and watch out for are falls when the climber is too far to the right or left in relationship to the toprope anchor, which

A discussion and demonstration on proper falling technique is appropriate for novices— feet wide, hanging in the harness, arms outstretched to brace against the rock, not grabbing the rope.

result in a swing or pendulum across the rock face; and falls when there is too much slack in the rope. Remember, if using a dynamic rope with a lot of rope in the system, rope stretch can be substantial (dynamic ropes stretch approximately 10 percent even in a toprope fall). When a climber is directly above the ground or a ledge, take particular care to

The right side of this toprope setup is clipped into a bolt that will act as a directional to prevent a falling climber from swinging.

ensure the rope is slightly under tension (especially if you are using a dynamic rope), to guard against rope stretch in the event of a fall.

A directional can be used to prevent a swing in the event of a fall. A directional is a separate piece of gear placed below and to the right or left of the main anchor. For example, if the start of the route is 20 feet to the right of the toprope anchor, and the climber falls near the bottom, he will swing 20 feet to the left during the fall (or even hit the ground). A solid piece placed directly in line above the start would be a directional, preventing the swing. When the climber reaches the piece, he simply unclips and continues to the top. As the climber is being lowered, he re-clips into the directional so that the climb is ready for the next climber.

Other Considerations

Climbing sites can be the habitat for things that sting and bite, both flora and fauna. Students should be informed of the hazard and given strategies to avoid an unpleasant encounter.

Weather is another hazard that must be considered. Instructors should check the forecast prior to the work day to ensure they and their students are adequately prepared for whatever weather conditions the day may bring. An excellent resource for regional and spot forecasts anywhere in the United States is the National Weather Service website: www.weather.gov.

CHAPTER 11

Top- or Base-Site Management for a Single Pitch

If an observer took a snapshot of recreational climbing teams around the country, he might begin to think that single pitch climbing has a default pattern. First, most climbers establish the climb; it is either led or the anchor is assembled and the toprope is tossed down from the top. The climber and the belayer are on the ground at the beginning and the end of the climb. Belaying seems to universally happen with the rope having been redirected through the anchor, and the belayer uses his or her own body as a counterweight, belaying directly off the belay loop. After the climb is over, someone has to clean the anchor.

It is inarguable that this single pitch paradigm predominates the climbing community, but instructors should appreciate that just because this arrangement is typical, it is not the only way to work a climb. In fact, many veteran instructors find the opposite arrangement, where the belayer lowers the climber down from the top of the climb, to be the most common arrangement in single pitch outings. For a professional instructor, neither arrangement should become the default setting. Every single outing, every crag, and every student requires a thorough instructor to make a choice: "Shall I work at the top of this climb, or shall I work at the bottom?" The goal of this chapter is to inventory all the options an instructor has when working in a single pitch setting, divulge the tools that are necessary to enable those options, and explore the criteria that an instructor would use to make an appropriate choice for his or her students.

Top-Managed Sites

Working at the top of a climb has many obvious advantages. For one thing, it may be the only way to work the crag. Many climbs are located along sea cliffs and riverbanks, on the rims of a canyon or cave, or at the top of a multi-pitch climbing area. For these kinds of climbing areas, the base of the climb is either inaccessible (hundreds of feet away), or there is water lapping against the bottom of the cliff. In each case, the climbing team will have to approach the top of the climb, build an anchor, lower a climber down, and have the climber climb back to the top.

When the instructor does have a choice, however, between the top and the bottom of a climb, there are still clear advantages to the top.

- The entire climbing team is rarely in danger of rockfall in an area accessed from the top.

- There is 50 percent less rope in the system, compared to a base site, minimizing rope elongation.

- Some climbers like climbing to the instructor.

- Belaying from the top allows an instructor to use an entire rope length when leading, opening longer pitches and huge stretches of terrain.

- The instructor can usually see the anchor system the entire time, monitoring components, sharp edges, and other users.

- An instructor already at the top of the climb can immediately clean the anchor, making the top site a more efficient way to work.

- The top site opens up programming options like rappelling.

A top-managed site at Joshua Tree National Park, California.

AMGA Single Pitch Instructor James Pierson top-manages a climber from a cliff in Washington's Larrabee State Park. Instructors working on a sea cliff have no choice but to work from the top.

TIM PAGE

There are clearly disadvantages to the top site as well. It is difficult or impossible to see climbers from above on many crags, and coaching individual moves is difficult. The climber's rope always goes over the edge when belaying from above, so sharp edges are particularly troublesome. Many cliff-top ecosystems are fragile and should not be unnecessarily impacted. Lastly, the cliff's edge is always close by, so instructors have to build technical systems to protect themselves and closely supervise participants who may try to venture too close to a precipice.

Because of these advantages and disadvantages in top-site work, instructors may find themselves preferring the top site for low-ratio work, especially in areas where lead climbing is the most common way to access the anchor. If there are only one or two students to manage, it is an efficient way to work.

When establishing a top site, instructors need to select an anchor and a stance that allows them to mitigate risks when approaching the cliff's edge (with a tether of some sort), recognizing that the space between the anchor and the cliff's edge is about to become a busy place. Instructors will be moving back and forth, students will be entering the system, rappels will be rigged, ropes will be stacked, etc. Instructors come to think of this area in front of the anchor as the "workspace," and that is an appropriate way to think of it. As a workspace, it should be clear of all superfluous equipment and personal items. As a workspace, tools should be logically arranged for easy access, or intentionally stowed. As a workspace, the things that happen there should have the tone of work: intentional, careful, and diligent. Students will need to be carefully instructed about where to stand and when and how it's okay to approach the cliff's edge.

Base-Managed Sites

Working from the base of the cliff has distinct advantages: There is no danger of anyone falling off the edge of the cliff, belayers are easily supervised, and climbers can be seen and coached on their way up the route. Recreational climbers will be most familiar with this arrangement, and it is most likely the system that they will default to using on their own, with friends, or in climbing gyms.

But hazards do exist for base-managed sites, such as rockfall and dropped gear. If the climbs are long, there is more rope in the system, so rope stretch can be a big hazard, particularly if a dynamic rope is being used for toproping.

Because of these advantages and disadvantages in base-site work, instructors may find themselves preferring the base site for high-ratio instruction. Groups can cheer on their friends, the outing has a social atmosphere, and multiple climbing teams can be supervised simultaneously. Furthermore, each climbing team can employ up to four student roles, so no one needs to sit idly by, waiting for their turn to do something. For any given climbing rope, one student will climb, one will belay, one can be a backup belayer, and one can serve as a ground anchor.

When should a ground anchor be used? If both the climber and belayer are roughly the same body weight and the terrain at the base of the cliff is flat, a ground anchor is unnecessary. But if the climber outweighs the belayer by more than 40 percent, a ground anchor should always be considered. A severe weight discrepancy will be even more obvious in low-friction setups, like overhangs. But friction, from a climber's body on a low-angled slab, or directional pieces that redirect the toprope, or the rope running over the rock itself, will help mitigate

The Ground Anchor

The worst accident I (BG) have had in thirty-five years of rock climbing happened when I was belaying in a toprope situation without a ground anchor. I was belaying from the base of the climb in a relaxed position about 15 feet out from the base of the cliff. Between the ledge I was belaying from and the cliff itself was a deep chimney. My partner was climbing on a toprope and suddenly fell while attempting an overhang about 50 feet above me. He swung wildly in the air. I easily caught the fall and locked off my belay device in the brake position, but I was pulled off my stance, swinging 15 feet straight into the wall like a pendulum. I braced for the impact with an outstretched leg and sustained a severely sprained ankle. A simple ground anchor would have prevented this accident. Belaying accidents are common, and in almost every case, they have the same element: no ground anchor.

This belayer is using a large block of rock for a ground anchor, ensuring she won't budge if the climber falls.

a severe difference in weight. Ground anchors rarely hurt anything. It is especially important to establish a ground anchor for the belayer in uneven terrain, particularly if the belay stance is perched high on top of boulders, or is some distance away from the base of the cliff.

A good system to rig a ground anchor is to start with the belayer tying in to the end of the rope. Not only does this "close" the rope system, but it allows the belayer to use the climbing rope to connect to a ground anchor with a clove hitch, which can be easily adjusted to suit the stance.

Natural anchors are obvious choices for ground anchors, like a sling or cordelette around a tree or a large block of rock. A single bomber cam or nut in a crack will also suffice. A seated student is an excellent choice for a ground anchor, especially if vegetation has been heavily impacted or other options are not available. The ground anchor student should be given a comfortable seat, like on top of a backpack.

The belayer in a toprope scenario will be pulled in a line directly to the toprope anchor master point, so he or she should be anchored and braced accordingly. Ideally the ground anchor will be low and directly behind or beneath the belayer or just slightly to the side. Remembering the ABCs may be helpful: anchor, belayer, climber. There should be a straight line between the anchor, the belayer, and the direction of pull created by the climber.

Belaying

Whether at the top-managed site or the base-managed site, belaying is a skill performed by students and instructors alike. It doesn't matter who is belaying or what they are belaying with, belaying is a very serious responsibility. It is a skill that instructors must understand, teach, and supervise.

All belaying has three irreducible principles that comprise the grounding theory of belaying; all the techniques discussed in this text will invoke these three key principles.

- The brake hand never leaves the rope.
- The hand transition should be made in a position of strength.
- The body should be positioned comfortably and sustainably.

Even before the popularization of manufactured belay devices, these principles were apparent. From device to device, the fundamental principles never changed. The hip belay was one of the original forms of the belay, and the principles used to make it work also apply to modern belay devices.

BELAY DEVICES

Today there is a wide variety of belay devices available. The most commonly used belay device is a tube or slot device (with two slots so it can be used for both belaying and rappelling on a doubled rope). A bight of rope is threaded through one of the slots in the belay device and clipped into a locking carabiner attached to the belay loop on the front of the belayer's harness. When the two strands of rope (one going to the climber, one to

Black Diamond ATC belay device.

Black Diamond ATC XP in high-friction mode with the teeth on the braking side.

The "Dreaded" Hip Belay

I (BG) began climbing before the advent of the belay device. Back in the 1970s we used the "hip belay" technique to catch a fall, which was simply wrapping the rope around your waist to generate enough friction to stop a fall. Catching a climber on a big "whipper" was painful indeed, and I often ended a hard day of climbing with a black streak singed across the back of my waistline.

To take in rope, start with the brake hand at your hip and the guide, or "feel," hand extended.

To take up slack, the brake hand goes out as the guide hand comes in.

The guide hand reaches above the brake hand and pinches the rope . . .

. . . so that the brake hand can slide back.

In the event of a fall, the brake hand brings the rope in front of the waist for maximum friction.

Standard Climbing Signals

A methodical systems check along with proper use of the universal climbing signals are integral parts of climbing. Ambiguity in the use of climbing signals has led to many tragic accidents, simply because of lack of communication between the climber and belayer. One infamous tragedy occurred at a popular ice climbing area, in a toprope setup, when the climber reached the top of the climb (at the top of the cliff) and the anchor. The climber yelled, "I'm OK!" but the belayer thought he heard, "Off belay." The belayer unclipped the rope from the belay device and took the climber off belay, thinking he was going to walk off the top. The climber leaned back to be lowered and fell to his death.

On a base-managed toprope climb, it's important to be vigilant at the transition from the climb up to the lower down. This is where most accidents due to improper communication and climbing signals occur. There should be no ambiguity. Many instructors hold onto the strand of rope that goes back down to the belayer until sure that the belayer has heard the command and is in the brake position and ready to hold weight. In most cases the instructor will be within visual contact, so in addition to hearing the verbal commands, the instructor should also look down and visually verify that the belayer is being attentive, with the brake hand in the proper position, alert and ready to lower in a controlled manner. In situations where climbing with other parties around, it's best to include the belayer's name in the signal (e.g., "Off belay, Bob.") to prevent confusion.

Here are the standardized climbing signals used in many climbing schools:

On belay?: Climber to belayer, "Am I on belay?"

Belay on: Belayer to climber, "The belay is on."

Climbing: Climber to belayer, "I'm beginning the climb."

Climb on: Belayer to climber, "Go ahead and start climbing; I have you on belay."

Up rope: Climber to belayer, "There is too much slack in my rope. Take up some of the slack." (Too much slack in the belay rope will mean a longer fall. Remember that rope stretch also contributes to the total distance of a fall, especially when there is a lot of rope out in a toprope scenario.)

Slack: Climber to belayer, "Give me some slack, the rope is too tight."

Tension (or Take): Climber to belayer, "Take all the slack out of the rope and pull it tight; I am going to hang all my body weight on the rope." (This could be a situation where the climber simply wants to rest by hanging in the harness while weighting the rope, or a toprope situation where the climber is getting ready to be lowered back down a climb.) Be careful with the word "take" as it can be misheard as "slack" or "safe."

Tension on (or I've got you): Belayer to climber, "I've taken the rope tight, and my brake hand is now locked off in the brake position, ready to hold all your weight."

Lower me (or Ready to lower): Climber to belayer, "I'm in the lowering position [feet wide, good stance, sitting in the harness, weighting the rope, and leaning back], and I'm ready to be lowered."

Lowering: Belayer to climber, "I'm proceeding to lower you."

Off belay: Climber to belayer, "I'm safe. You can unclip the rope from your belay device and take me off belay." (Never take someone off belay unless this signal has been heard. The universal contract between belayer and climber is that the belayer must never take the climber off belay unless the climber gives the belayer the "off belay" command.)

Belay off: Belayer to climber, "I've unclipped the rope from my belay device and have taken you off belay."

That's me!: Climber to belayer, "You've taken up all the slack in the rope and the rope is now tight to my harness."

Watch me!: Climber to belayer, "Heads up! Be attentive with the belay—there is a good chance I'm going to fall right here!"

Falling!: Climber to belayer, "I'm actually falling, go to your brake position and lock off the rope to catch my fall!" (A fall can happen so fast that the climber might not be able to shout this signal during a short fall, but it helps the belayer react more quickly, especially in situations where the belayer can't see the climber.)

ROCK!: Climber to belayer and others below, "I've dislodged a rock and it's now freefalling below me—watch out below!" (The equivalent signal to "fore!" in golf, "ROCK!" should also be yelled when the climber drops a piece of equipment.)

the belayer's brake hand) are held parallel, in front of the belay device, there is little friction, but when the brake strand is held at a 180-degree angle relative to the strand going to the climber, the device affords maximum friction, making it relatively easy to hold the force of a falling climber.

So long as a belay method adheres to the three fundamental principles of belay, there are many techniques acceptable for a sound belay. Along with loyalty to the fundamental principles, good belaying technique effectively manages rope slack, requires maintaining a brake hand on the brake strand side of the rope, and generates enough friction to stop a fall and properly lower a climber.

Over the last decade advances in technology have allowed manufacturers to produce thinner

ropes, and belay devices have evolved along with the ropes. When buying a belay device, check the manufacturer's specifications and make sure it's appropriate for the diameter of the climbing ropes being used. The most popular tube device is the Black Diamond ATC (tongue in cheek for Air Traffic Controller), which also comes in a more versatile version with teeth on one side (the ATC XP) that gives the belayer two options: a regular friction mode when the brake strand is on the non-teeth side, or roughly twice the amount of friction when the brake strand is on the teeth side.

Assisted braking devices (ABDs) have become popular for toprope belaying. The most popular models include the Petzl Grigri and the Trango Cinch. These devices have a mechanical lever that

Petzl Grigri in lowering mode.

Trango Cinch in lowering mode.

should engage during a fall. Once weighted, the braking lever pinches the brake strand quite hard, so the device has a handle that must be opened to release the tension. When lowering a climber, the belayer must simultaneously manipulate the mechanical lever with the handle with one hand, while maintaining friction and controlling the speed of the lower with the brake hand. These coordinated movements mean that ABDs are far from foolproof, and many accidents have occurred with ABDs, typically when someone is being lowered. The cardinal rule to teach with any belay device is this: Never take your brake hand off the

rope! After all, it's the first fundamental principle of belay.

With any belay device, read the manufacturer's guidelines carefully, and seek proper instruction from an AMGA certified instructor if you have any doubts about how to use the device or the proper technique to use when belaying with the device.

Belaying in a Base-Managed Site

Whether using an ATC or an ABD, the following sequence best adheres to the fundamental principles of belay in a base-managed site.

The PBUS (pull, brake, under, slide) method of belaying on a toprope. Start by clipping the rope into the slot in the belay device closest to the spine side of the carabiner and orient the rope so that the brake side is down.

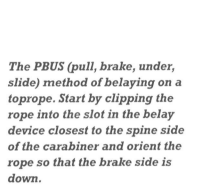

To take up rope, pull the rope up with your brake hand (palm down) as you simultaneously pull the rope down with the other hand . . .

. . . then brake the rope down under your belay device.

Take your non-brake hand and firmly grasp the rope directly under the belay device . . .

. . . then slide your brake hand up against that hand and repeat the process. This technique is easy to learn and maintains a firm brake position on the rope at all times. In a fall, remember that the brake position is down.

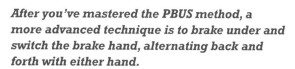

After you've mastered the PBUS method, a more advanced technique is to brake under and switch the brake hand, alternating back and forth with either hand.

Two-Rope Toprope Setups

When rigging long topropes of more than half a single rope length, two ropes can be tied together using knots like the double fisherman's knot or figure eight bend knot. With such a huge amount of rope out between the climber and the belayer, rope stretch is a major concern, especially when using dynamic ropes. Remember that even a short fall in a toprope situation will stretch a dynamic rope about 10 percent, so tighten up the rope when belaying someone just off the ground, or just above a ledge.

Here are two methods that can be used to deal with the knot joining the two ropes. The simple solution, and also the best if there will not be a stance for the climber to stop at, avoids the knot pass altogether. With the knot joining the two ropes at the anchor, tie a figure eight loop and attach it to the climber's belay loop with two locking carabiners (gates opposed and reversed). When the climber reaches the anchor, the knot will be just above the belayer's device, so no knot pass is required.

Another solution is to use two belay devices. The climber ties in to the end of the rope as usual. The belayer anticipates the knot pass and has a second belay device clipped to his belay loop, at the ready. When the knot reaches the belayer, the belayer alerts the climber to find a good stance, then ties a backup knot (overhand loop) on the brake hand side of the belay device. The belayer steps forward to create a bit of slack, then clips the rope into the second belay device on the climber's side of the knot, leaving the first belay device clipped in. If another person is available, that person can assist the belayer simply by holding the rope with both hands under a little tension above the belay device as the belayer accomplishes this. When the climber reaches the anchor, the belayer lowers the climber until the knot is almost to the belay device, and the process is reversed: The climber takes a stance, the belayer unclips the second belay device (first double-checking that the first belay device is still clipped in and has the backup knot), then unties the backup knot and lowers the climber as normal. Knot-passing techniques are something that should be practiced with a qualified instructor.

Backup Belayers

The purpose of the backup belayer is simple: In case the primary belayer loses control of the brake, the backup belayer, holding the brake strand side of the rope, holds the rope to prevent a fall, essentially backing up the belayer's brake hand. For first-time belayers it is appropriate for the instructor to be the backup belayer. For intermediate-level students who have demonstrated proficiency in belaying techniques, other students are commonly used for backup belayers. As an instructor, when you demonstrate a climb with a student belayer, adding another student as a backup belayer gives you an added layer of protection.

To properly back up a belay, the backup belayer should be positioned behind and, if possible, below the belayer's brake hand, so that the backup belayer's hands can activate the brake position of the belayer's device if needed. The backup belayer takes in or feeds out rope as needed, leaving enough slack so that the rope is not being tugged from the belayer's brake hand, or in any way impeding the belayer's ability to manage the belay. If the belayer

Backup belayer in action. Note that the backup belayer is providing a hip belay for extra security. This may be required in places where an in-line belay backup is difficult to achieve.

JASON D. MARTIN

Here a climber provides a "meat anchor" for the belayer. The backup belayer provides an in-line backup belay.

RON FUNDERBURKE

loses control of the brake hand, the backup belayer essentially takes over the braking role. The critical juncture for the backup belayer is when the climber reaches the anchor and transitions into being lowered. The backup belayer can also help the belayer by managing the free end of the rope, preventing any tangles from reaching the belayer.

Some instructors run the rope from the belayer's brake strand through a carabiner on a ground anchor behind the belayer, redirecting the rope back up to a backup belayer. When done properly, this keeps the rope low and in the braking plane, which allows the backup belayer to stand or change locations without compromising the effectiveness of the backup. This redirect technique is also helpful if the instructor is the backup belayer. The instructor can stand in front of the belayer to visually monitor the belayer and climber at the same time while keeping the brake strand in the braking plane.

Another backup technique is the use of a "catastrophe knot." This is simply an overhand knot tied on the rope on the brake strand side of the belayer's belay device. The catastrophe knot can be used if, for some reason, the instructor needs to walk away from the backup belayer role momentarily. If the climber falls and the belayer loses control, the overhand knot will jam in the belay device, preventing a catastrophic fall.

Belaying from the Top

The method preferred by most professional instructors when belaying from the top of the cliff is the direct belay. In a direct belay the belay device is

A direct belay with a Munter hitch. In this sequence the belayer's right hand is the brake hand. The starting position (position 1) is with the brake hand at the top and the guide (or feel) hand lower (left photo). Pull the rope down with the brake hand as the guide hand goes up (center). Feeding the rope up toward the carabiner with the guide hand, rather than pulling the rope down tightly with just the brake hand, lessens kinking of the rope. Now take the non-brake hand and grasp the rope below the brake hand (right). This is both the brake position and lowering position. Unlike a tube device, the maximum friction with a Munter hitch is when the two rope strands are parallel to each other. To continue the hand sequence, return to position 1.

The direct belay. A Grigri is clipped directly to the master point.

Detail of a direct belay setup. The belayer is anchored with a clove hitch, and the Grigri is clipped directly to the anchor master point.

clipped directly to the anchor, and in the event of a fall, the anchor, not the belayer, bears the brunt of the fall and holds the climber's weight.

Using a standard belaying device, like an ATC, is not recommended for use in a direct belay, because unless the device is positioned below waist level, the braking position will be very awkward, and the instructor will be in a weak and dangerous position to hold a fall. If the master point is above waist level, the Munter hitch works well, since the braking

position for maximum friction is when the two strands of rope are parallel to each other, with the brake position down below the carabiner, not above it. Belaying with a Munter also allows instructors the option of positioning themselves some distance away from the Munter belay carabiner due to the maximum braking power achieved with both rope strands parallel to each other.

A commonly used method for a direct belay is to use an assisted braking device (e.g., Petzl Grigri

Not for Instructors

Recreational climbers tend to use two systems that have limited applications for professional instructors. The first is the indirect belay, which is a fancy way of saying a belay directly off the harness. The second is the redirected belay, a technique where the rope runs from the belayer at the top through carabiners at the anchor and then back down to the climber.

The indirect belay is considered to be indirect because the force of a fall is not directly placed on the anchor. Instead, the belayer's body takes a portion of the force, which depending on the position and stance could be a large portion or a small portion.

An indirect belay is a poor choice for an instructor because you are "in the system," frozen in the position that you set up. This makes it difficult to see and coach your climber. Additionally, if something goes wrong, it is difficult, technical, and time consuming to escape the belay.

A redirected belay is a similar technique, but instead of running directly to the climber's belay loop, the rope is first redirected through carabiners in the anchor. The problems with the redirected belay are similar to those with the indirect belay. The instructor can become stuck in the system, unable to coach a climber below, and this belay also is difficult to escape in the event of an emergency.

In addition to the preceding, there are two other problems implicit in a redirected belay. First, when a heavy climber lowers, the belayer can be pulled up into the system. And second, this system puts more force on the anchor.

A redirected belay puts more force on the anchor by creating a 2:1 pulley system at the master point. Such a system requires an equal amount of weight on both strands of rope to remain static. In other words, if a 200-pound person falls on a redirected belay, you will have to counteract that weight with an additional 200 pounds, placing 400 pounds directly onto the anchor.

While some might argue that there are legitimate reasons to use an indirect or a redirect belay, there are few legitimate reasons to use these techniques in a single pitch instructional scenario.

or Trango Cinch) or autoblocking device (e.g., ATC Guide or Petzl Reverso) clipped directly to the master point of the anchor.

The advantage of a Grigri or similar device is that in the event of a fall, the Grigri simply locks off, and the anchor holds the climber's weight. When using a Grigri in the direct belay mode, take care when the device is close to the rock, as anything that presses against the handle (i.e., the rock) will release the braking mechanism. Be sure to position the handle away from the rock.

Remember, a regular ATC or similar non-autoblocking device is not recommended for use in a direct belay if the master point is at or above the belayer's waist level, as the braking position would be very awkward.

Lowering from a Top-Managed Site

There are several lowering methods that are quick and easy to rig. Before lowering someone, make sure the system is closed and the rope is properly flaked at the instructor's feet. Climbing instructors should choose an ergonomic stance that will not put them in an awkward position, and will allow visual contact with students all the way to the ground. If the anchor is not close enough to the edge to allow this, a tether or anchor extension should be incorporated into the system.

Lowering with a Munter Hitch

The rope is flaked at the instructor's feet, so if there are any tangles, they can be handily dealt with. Note that the tail of the rope sitting on top of the rope stack will soon be tied to a student. Therefore, wherever that rope goes, the student will have to follow that same path while approaching the cliff's edge to be lowered. Make sure the student has a clear avenue to the cliff's edge once on belay. Toss the rope to the student and instruct them to tie in. Next, use a locking carabiner designed for use with a Munter hitch on the anchor. Back it up with an autoblock clipped to a locking carabiner at the instructor's belay loop, and begin formal belay commands with the student. One advantage of the Munter hitch for lowering is that an instructor does not have to be at the Munter carabiner to effectively manage the braking position, since the optimal friction is when both rope strands are parallel to each other. This allows an instructor some flexibility; he or she can tether as far away from the Munter as desired while maintaining an effective belay.

Lowering with an Assisted Braking Device

When given the option, many Single Pitch Instructors will lower a student using a Grigri. Since it has a built-in braking system, there is no need to back

A Grigri in lowering mode with the brake strand redirected using the Petzl Freino carabiner, which is specifically designed for this application.

it up with an autoblock. Petzl actually sells a carabiner, called the Freino, that has a special gate on the side of the carabiner for the brake strand to be clipped into, to facilitate lowering. Without the special carabiner, an instructor can redirect the brake strand back up through a separate carabiner clipped to the master point (or, on a cordelette anchor, up to the shelf). The big advantage of the Grigri is that once the rope is clipped in, it can be used for lowering (just remember to redirect the brake strand!) or belaying (as the climber climbs back up), and it's all set to rig a 3:1 hauling system if a climber needs some assistance on the way back up.

A Grigri rigged for lowering with the brake strand redirected through a carabiner clipped to the master point.

Using an Autoblock Knot as a Backup When Lowering

Whenever lowering a student with a belay device other than an assisted braking device, it's best to back up the brake hand with an autoblock knot clipped to a locking carabiner attached to the instructor's belay loop.

Some instructors call the autoblock the "third hand," because if the brake hand releases when lowering or rappelling, the autoblock grabs the brake strand of the rope. The autoblock adds an extra level of security, especially when there are tangles in the rope that require untangling.

If the stance at the anchor does not allow a clear field of vision down the cliff, to watch climbers while lowering, then instructors can rig the rope direct belay system to position themselves at the edge to maintain visual contact. Instructors should always strive for visual contact with their students whenever belaying or lowering.

The belayer is ready to lower the climber with a Munter hitch on a locking carabiner clipped to the master point, backed up with an autoblock clipped to a locking carabiner attached to the belayer's belay loop.

Lowering with a Munter hitch and an autoblock. The belayer is holding an autoblock backup that's clipped with a locking carabiner to his belay loop.

Here the instructor is positioned at the cliff's edge to maintain visual contact with the climber being lowered using a munter hitch at the anchor's BHK master point. The instructor is using a Grigri on the white fixed line (instructor tether) to allow for adjustable positioning. Note the backup knot tied on the fixed rope on the brake strand side of the Grigri. The instructor's brake hand on the lowering rope is backed up with an autoblock knot attached to his belay loop.

CHAPTER 12

Rappelling

The first question the instructor needs to answer is "why rappel?" Is there an easier way to descend from the top of the cliff? Would lowering be more efficient? Can the risks be properly managed? The most common reasons for rappelling are to teach novices the fundamental skills of rappelling or to provide students with an experience. Every recreational climber needs to know the fundamentals of rappelling; it is one of the cornerstone skills of technical rock climbing. Additionally, rappelling can be an impactful activity. It is an activity where students take complete responsibility for managing their own risk. Properly facilitated, it can be a great tool for building self-confidence and generating a sense of accomplishment. The instructor should have clear goals for conducting the activity and should avoid treating rappelling like an amusement ride.

Teaching Rappelling

Site Selection

Site selection is important to teach a novice rappelling technique. Select a site that has a comfortable, flat area on top without a drastic transition from the horizontal to the vertical. The ideal site should have a high master point for the rappel and belay anchor and a flat "desktop" area that extends at least 10 feet back from the edge of the cliff, be free of loose rocks, and have a rounded, gradual edge for a comfortable transition to a wall that is angled slightly less than vertical. The site should also provide a good stance for the instructor, where he or she can coach and model while maintaining visual and

verbal contact with the student during the entire rappel. The cliff face should be free of loose rock and uniformly flat, not riddled with cracks, and without corners or overhangs. The base should have a nice flat landing area without boulders, bushes, or trees.

Rigging for Contingencies

In the institutional setting all students are belayed when they are learning to rappel. A good instructional system anticipates any potential problems that may occur during a rappel and uses a rigging system that is ready to remedy any problem.

Student Rappel Belays

Belaying students while rappelling can be done from the base or from the top of the cliff. The technique used at the base is called the fireman's belay. This technique requires the instructor to be at the bottom of the rappel. Holding the rappel rope, the instructor can stop the rappeller's progress by forcefully pulling down on the rope. When the instructor pulls down on the rope and applies tension, the rappeller will stop—it's not possible to move down the rope when it is under tension. This technique requires the instructor to be on high alert, prepared to arrest a fall the moment it happens. Failure to react quickly can lead to loss of control of the belay, with catastrophic consequences. The fireman's belay should be limited to situations where there are two instructors present: one to perform the belay and one to monitor and coach the students on top. It is

Instructor-belayed rappel rigged from a high master point.

Elevators

C are needs to be taken to avoid having the master point pinned to the ground once the student has weighted the system and gone over the edge. A low master point has two disadvantages. It makes the system difficult to manage for the instructor, and it makes the transition over the edge far more demanding for the novice rappeller. The SAR community uses a "high redirect" (aka an elevator) to deal with this; it's also an elegant solution to the problem for the climbing instructor. A simple way to create an elevator is to use a pack to prop up the master point; however, the use of trees or terrain features are a much more effective way. With a little creativity there is no reason to grovel in the dirt while managing a belayed rappel.

not a recommended belay technique when dealing with novices or when facilitating an experience. Assisting or rescuing a student in mid-rappel is highly problematic with this technique.

The preferred method for students who will be rappelling for the first time is to provide a belay from above. The system can be rigged using one or two ropes. One line is the rappel line; the other is the belay line. If the length of the rappel is less than half the rope length, the system can be rigged with a single rope. One end is tied to the belayer, and the other end goes to the ground and includes a stopper knot. If the rappel is more than half a rope length, two ropes are required. The rappel rope is attached to the anchor with a Munter/mule combination, which is releasable under tension. The rappeller is tied into the belay rope and belayed on a direct belay with a Munter hitch off the anchor. The belay rope is neatly stacked at the instructor's feet.

It is recommended that an assisted braking device *not* be used in this situation, for a couple of reasons. First, it is difficult to manage the ABD and maintain visual contact with the rappeller. Second, and more importantly, it is nearly impossible to provide slack to the belay line smoothly as the rappeller progresses. Under this circumstance, the student isn't actually rappelling; it becomes more of a lower.

Sometimes the rappeller encounters a problem (like long hair or clothing stuck in the rappel device, or a knot in the rappel rope) and can't continue. As always, seek the nontechnical solution first. If one cannot be found, fix the problem by doing the following:

1. Tie off the Munter on the belay line with a mule knot and overhand backup.

2. Release the mule knot on the rappel line and give the rappeller some slack.

3. Have the rappeller fix the problem (e.g., take the hair out of the device).

4. Re-tie the mule knot with an overhand backup.

5. Release the mule knot on the belay line and continue belaying the rappel.

The Instructor Rappel Backup

Instructors should manage personal risk by using a backup when rappelling. In the old days the most common method for a rappel backup was using a prusik knot on the ropes above the rappel device, connected to the harness with a sling. The non-brake hand would cup the prusik knot and hold it in a loosened position during the rappel, allowing it to slide down the rope. Letting go of the knot allowed it to slide up and grab onto the ropes,

Extended Master Point for Belay Strand

The belay line on a releasable rappel should always be extended so that the carabiners don't pinch the rope between one another. One way to do this is to use a runner basketed through the master point. By tying an overhand knot in the basketed sling, two additional redundant master points are created. Another way is to mule off the rappel line on one locking carabiner, while belaying the student off two enchained locking carabiners. And yet another way is to use a double loop figure eight knot, making each loop a different length, provided an appropriate diameter anchor rope is used and that it is not placed on an abrasive surface.

Detail of belayed rappel setup, rigged for contingencies. The rappeller is rappelling on the rope in the foreground, tied to the master point with a Munter/mule combination, which is releasable under tension. The belayer is belaying with the direct belay technique using a Munter hitch from an extended master point, created by basketing a double-length (48-inch) nylon runner through the anchor's two-loop master point, then tying it with an overhand knot for redundancy. The Munter/ mule/overhand combo is one ugly knot, but it's easily releasable under tension, and that's the beauty of it.

At this site the distance of the rappel is over 100 feet, so the system is rigged with two ropes. The yellow rope is the rappel rope, attached to the anchor with a Munter/mule/overhand combination. The blue rope is the belay line. Note how the instructor has created multiple master points with the doubled yellow nylon sling.

Here one bi-pattern rope is used for a releasable belayed rappel scenario. A BHK master point is rigged with a low-stretch (red) rope. The instructor is attached to a tether (red rope) with a Grigri. The striped orange dynamic rope held by the instructor is the belay line, and the rope at the bottom is the other half of the bi-pattern dynamic rope, serving as the rappel rope, attached to the anchor with a Munter/mule/overhand combination. By basketing the yellow nylon sling through the two-loop BHK master point and tying an overhand knot, the instructor has created two additional master points.

Without staggered master points, things can get clustered in a releasable rappel scenario.

stopping the rappel. There are two drawbacks with this method. One is that for the prusik to lock off, it must hold all the rappeller's weight. The second is that once it is weighted, the rappeller must remove all body weight from the prusik knot in order for it to be released, not an easy task on a free-hanging rappel.

The modern rappel backup utilizes the autoblock knot, rigged below the rappel device. There are two distinct advantages with this method. One is that for the autoblock knot to grab, it only needs to hold a very small percentage of the rappeller's weight, since it is on the braking side of the device, and the device itself is holding most of the weight and providing most of the friction. It is essentially

like a brake hand squeezing and gripping the rope, and for that reason some instructors refer to it as the "third hand." The second big advantage of the autoblock method is that it is releasable under tension (i.e., when weighted and grabbing onto the rope). While rappelling down, simply form a circle with the thumb and forefinger (like the OK sign) and push the autoblock down while descending, allowing the rope to freely slide through the knot. When released, the autoblock knot rides up and grabs onto the rope, like the brake hand squeezing the rope. Releasing the autoblock, even when weighted, is as simple as sliding it back down and holding it in the "open" position. It's a beautiful thing, and easy to rig.

Left: Black Diamond ATC XP rigged for rappelling with a three-wrap autoblock backup clipped to the leg loop with a locking carabiner.

Bottom: another view of how to rig an autoblock backup, here using a Black Diamond ATC rappel device and a three-wrap autoblock tied with 6mm nylon cord attached to the leg loop with a locking carabiner.

Not Foolproof

I (BG) conducted several tests over the last year with my autoblock rigged at my leg loop and my rappel device (ATC) at my belay loop. With someone giving me a fireman's belay to back me up, I flipped upside down to see if the autoblock would grab and hold. In three out of four tests, it failed to grip since it had ridden up against my ATC, and the rope kept sliding right through. It's not a foolproof backup.

When the technique was first introduced, the autoblock was attached to the rappeller's leg loop with a carabiner. The disadvantage of clipping the autoblock to a leg loop is that if for some reason the rappeller were to go unconscious and flip upside down, the autoblock would ride up and come in contact with the rappel device, which would prevent it from grabbing.

Also, recent harness leg loop buckle designs (particularly the Black Diamond trakFIT and Petzl "doubleback" buckle systems) can loosen when a carabiner is clipped into them and pulled outward.

If using an autoblock on a leg loop, make sure the harness buckle cannot be defeated by an outward pull, or better yet, use a harness with a fixed (no buckle) leg loop design. If you have a harness with one of these buckles and need to rappel off the belay loop, consider clipping your autoblock to the inside of the leg loop, opposite the buckle.

In recent years a more secure method has been developed: extending the rappel device with a sling attached to the harness, and rigging the autoblock clipped into the belay loop. One configuration is to rig a double-length sewn nylon sling threaded

Note where the carabiner sits on the harness. Rigging an autoblock backup from this position has the potential to unbuckle the leg loop.

JASON D. MARTIN

If you have a harness with suspect buckles, rig the autoblock backup from the inside of the leg loop.

JASON D. MARTIN

Rappelling **215**

Adam Fox demonstrates the proper use of an extended rappel device with autoblock backup. A double-length nylon runner is threaded through the harness tie-in points and tied with an overhand knot for redundancy. The rappel device is the Black Diamond ATC Guide in rappel mode. The autoblock knot is clipped to a locking carabiner attached to the belay loop.

through both tie-in points at the front of the harness and tied with an overhand knot, to gain redundancy at the sling. The preferred cordage is a nylon sling (18mm or $^{11}/_{16}$-inch width) over a thin (10mm) Dyneema sling for this application because nylon has a higher melting point. If the rappel rope is running across the sling, it could potentially create some heat due to the friction, which could damage the sling and reduce its breaking strength in later applications.

Managing the Risks— Avoiding Rappelling Accidents

When teaching rappelling to novice climbers, it is important to stress risk management. Although rappelling is a simple technique, statistically a high percentage of rappelling accidents end in a fatality. Analyzing rappelling accidents helps to understand what can go wrong and what to do to keep it from happening. Here is a look at the most common rappelling accident scenarios.

Scenario 1: Rappelling Off One or Both Ends of the Rope

This happens with some regularity, and almost every year there are several fatal rappelling accidents in America where someone simply rappelled off the end (or ends) of a rope. In the single pitch environment, it can happen when the ends are uneven on a double-rope rappel, especially if there is no middle mark. When the short end passes through the rappelling device, only one strand of the doubled rope remains in the device, and the climber's body weight rapidly pulls the rope through the rappel anchor, quickly dispatching the climber to the ground. To prevent this, *close the system* by tying stopper knots separately in both ends of the rope. Make sure that the stopper knot will jam in the rappel device that is being used.

Scenario 2: Not Clipping Both Strands of the Rope into the Carabiner on a Double-Rope Rappel

This is an easy mistake to make when not alert and double-checking the system. When visually inspecting the top of a tube-style device, it will appear as if both strands are properly threaded because the

Check and Check Again

I (BG) have done thousands of rappels in my climbing career, and one time I caught myself not clipping both strands on a double-rope rappel. Luckily for me I'd rigged an autoblock backup, and as I weighted the system, I noticed my error. If not for that autoblock backup, I probably wouldn't be writing this today.

device holds the bight of rope inside itself, even if the rope hasn't been clipped into the carabiner behind it. If only one strand makes it into the locking carabiner, when leaning back and weighting the rope, the climber will descend as rapidly as in the first scenario—and with equally injurious or fatal results. A good habit is to first tether in with a sling to the rappel anchor, rig the rappel device, then weight the rappel system and double-check everything before unclipping the tether. Rigging an autoblock backup is also a good idea.

Rappelling Systems Check

It is important to teach students how to go through a systematic mental checklist before rappelling. An acronym that facilitates the process is ABCDE. A is the rappel anchor. Take a look at the anchor, slings, chains, etc., and make sure the rappel rope is threaded properly through the anchor. The anchor should be redundant all the way to the point where the rope is threaded through the anchor. Do not rely on a single piece of gear in the anchor system, whether it is a single cord, sling, or rappel ring. B is for buckles on your harness—double-check to make sure they are buckled properly and doubled back appropriately. C is for carabiner. Make sure the locking carabiner that attaches the rappel device to the harness is being loaded properly on the long axis—and squeeze check to make sure that it is locked! D is for look down and see where the rope goes. Does it reach the ground? Or the next ledge? E is for the rope ends. Do they have stopper knots? Is the system closed?

Scenario 3:
Not Tethering to the Anchor

A sewn sling clipped to the anchor with a locking carabiner for a tether is all it takes to prevent this scenario. Using a daisy chain as a personal tether is not recommended, because if a carabiner is clipped into two adjacent loops, a weak and dangerous connection has been created. Better than a standard daisy chain with sewn pockets is the newer, modern version that consists of full runner-strength sewn loops, like the Metolius PAS (personal anchor system) or the Sterling Chain Reactor. These more versatile tethers also allow the rappel device to be extended away from the harness as described in the Instructor Rappel Backup. Again, a good habit is to weight the rappel device and check to make sure it's rigged properly and supports body weight before unclipping the tether from the anchor.

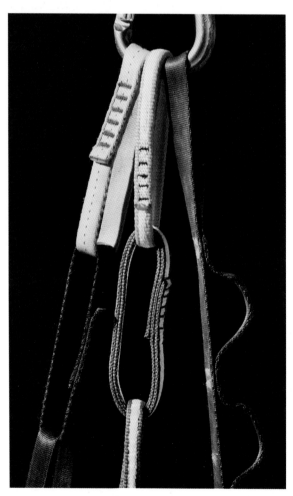

Tether comparison. Left to right: Sterling Chain Reactor, Metolius PAS, Black Diamond Daisy Chain.

A traditional daisy chain with bartacked pockets is not recommended for rappel extensions or as a personal tether, because if a carabiner is clipped into two loops, an extremely weak connection is created (3 kN or 674 lbs.).

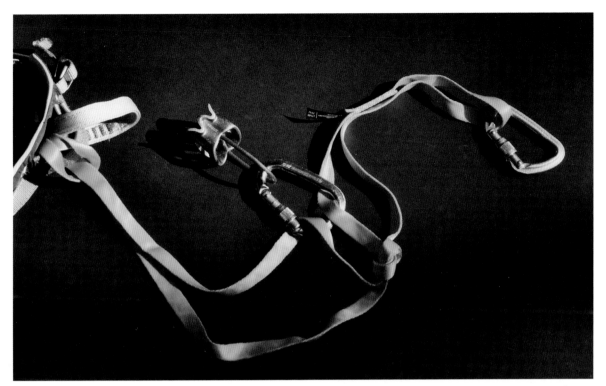

To rig a tether/rappel extension with a sling, start with a double-length (48-inch/120cm) sling and girth-hitch it through both tiein points on the harness. Tie an overhand knot about halfway down the length of the sling, adjusting the knot so that when it is clipped back into the harness belay loop with a locking carabiner, the length to the overhand knot is equalized. Clip the locking carabiner of the rappel device into both loops in the sling to make the sling itself redundant when it's clipped back into the harness belay loop.

Here my double-length (48-inch) Black Diamond 18mm nylon sling is rigged as a tether/extension. I (BG) girth-hitched the yellow sling through both harness tie-in points. I'd previously tied an overhand knot in the sling, and I then clipped the locking carabiner of my rappel device (a Petzl Reverso) into both loops in the sling. I rigged an autoblock backup with a Sterling Hollowblock and clipped it to my harness belay loop with a locking carabiner. After I double-check everything, I'll unclip the locking carabiner from the anchor and clip it back to my harness belay loop, adding redundancy to the sling.

CHAPTER 13

Basic Assistance and Rescue Skills

One of the many reasons that a student elects to take a course from a certified climbing instructor is that there is an unwritten agreement between the instructor and the student. The agreement is that if the student gets into trouble on the course, the instructor will be there to help the student get back out of trouble.

Certainly the word "trouble" could mean many different things. Examples include anything from forgetting one's water bottle in the car to suffering an injury. From a technical perspective in a single pitch environment, trouble commonly means that an individual is stuck somehow on a route. Following are several ways to get people unstuck and out of trouble.

Assistance from the Base

The first step in any assist scenario is to seek out the nontechnical solution. Coaching, encouraging, directing, or allowing gravity to take over are more efficient and expose both the instructor and student to fewer risks. When it becomes apparent that a nontechnical solution will not resolve the problem, it is time to incorporate more advanced techniques.

The basic assist skills presented below are most easily accomplished with an ABD, like a Grigri, and it is recommended that an ABD be used for belaying from both the base and top of the cliff, as it streamlines and facilitates these assist techniques. It is the right tool for the job and worth every extra ounce that it weighs over a traditional belay device. It is recommended that instructors learn the climber pickoff and the 3:1 raising system with a Grigri before trying it without one.

The Climber Pickoff

The "climber pickoff" is essentially the same technique used by the belayer to rescue a fallen lead climber who is injured and can't be lowered. The difference in a toprope situation is that there is a solid anchor system, not just the one piece of gear that held the leader's fall.

The climber pickoff utilizes a counterbalance ascension and rappel technique and requires minimal equipment. Basically the instructor ascends the rope to the climber, then rappels down with them.

All that is needed is the following equipment:

- 1 double-length (48-inch) sling
- 1 locking carabiner
- 1 prusik cord (6mm or 7mm soft nylon cord, 5 feet long, tied into a sling with a double fisherman's knot)

When belaying with a Grigri, follow these steps:

1. Start by tying a backup knot (overhand loop) on the brake strand side of the Grigri.

2. Tie a friction hitch (klemheist or prusik) with the prusik cord on the load strand going up to the climber, and attach the double-length sling to it with a locking carabiner.

3. Ascend the rope by sliding the friction hitch up, so that when the foot is placed in the sling the knee is bent at a 90-degree angle. A knot can be tied in the sling to shorten it as needed. Stand up in the sling, and as you straighten the leg, simultaneously pull the slack through the Grigri (pulling straight up on the brake strand) and hang in the harness off the Grigri. Alternate

standing up in the sling, then hanging in the harness, tight to the Grigri. About every 10 feet or so, tie a backup knot (overhand loop) on the brake strand side of the Grigri.

4. Upon reaching the climber, transfer the friction hitch from the instructor side of the rope onto the rope above the climber. The instructor then takes the double-length sling and threads it (basket style) through his or her belay loop and clips both ends of the sling to the locking carabiner attached to the friction hitch. Where the friction hitch is positioned will affect where

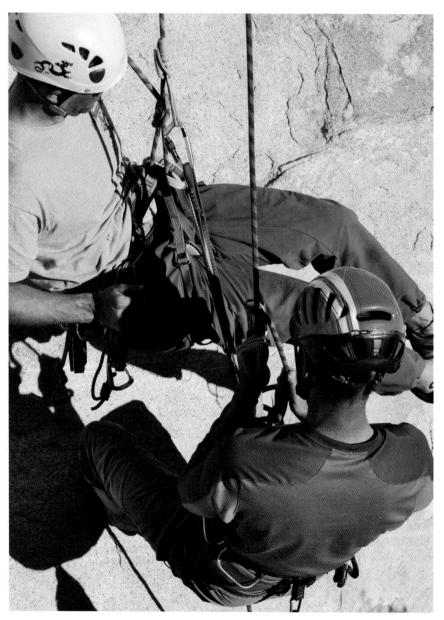

Counterbalance rappel using a Grigri after "picking off" a climber from the cliff.

the assisted climber will be positioned. If the friction hitch is high, the climber will remain at that position while rappelling. If the position of the friction hitch (klemheist or prusik) is just above the climber tie-in knot, the climber will move up and slightly above the instructor while descending.

5. Rappel with the Grigri, untying the backup knots as you descend.

Basic assistance skills will allow an instructor to assist a student if needed.

Rare Rescues

In over thirty years of professionally guiding thousands of clients in toprope situations, I (BG) have only had a few instances where I actually had to go up on the rock and bring a climber down—all of them being young kids who were overcome by fear and mentally lost control, afraid to lean back and weight the rope so they could be lowered back down. Having the knowledge and skills to go up the rope and bring a student down is important in case the instructor ever has to assist an injured student, even in a toprope situation.

If taking over someone else's belay and the belay strand is weighted, the sequence would be as follows:

1. Tie a backup knot (overhand loop) on the brake strand side of the belayer's belay device.

2. Clip a Grigri onto the rope between the backup knot and the belayer's belay device.

3. Tie a friction hitch (prusik or klemheist) on the load strand (going up to the climber) of the belayer's rope.

4. Thread (basket style) the double-length sling through the belayer's belay loop and attach it to the friction hitch with a locking carabiner.

5. Have the belayer give slack at the belay device—the tension will now be transferred to the friction hitch, with the belayer essentially becoming a ground anchor; the belayer then can unclip and remove the belay device.

6. Transfer the weight of the hanging climber from the belayer to the instructor's Grigri, by taking up all the slack in the rope and pulling upward on the brake strand side of the Grigri, using body weight as the anchor.

7. Unclip one end of the sling from the locking carabiner at the friction hitch.

8. Ascend the rope by sliding the friction hitch up, so that when the foot is placed in the sling the knee is bent at a 90-degree angle. A knot can be tied in the sling to shorten it as needed. Stand up in the sling, and as you straighten the leg, simultaneously pull the slack through the Grigri (pulling straight up on the brake strand) and hang in the harness off the Grigri. Alternate standing up in the sling, then hanging in the harness, tight to the Grigri. About every 10 feet

or so, tie a backup knot (overhand loop) on the brake strand side of the Grigri.

9. Upon reaching the climber, transfer the friction hitch from the instructor side of the rope onto the rope above the climber. The instructor then takes the double-length sling and threads it (basket style) through his or her belay loop, and clips both ends of the sling to the locking carabiner attached to the friction hitch. Where the friction hitch is positioned will affect where the assisted climber will be positioned. If the friction hitch is high, the climber will remain at that position while rappelling. If the position of the friction hitch (klemheist or prusik) is just above the climber tie-in knot, the climber will move up and slightly above the instructor while descending.

10. Rappel with the Grigri, untying the backup knots as you descend.

Assistance from the Top

Coaching

The best and easiest way to assist a climber who's climbing up to you from below is simply to position your belay stance where you'll be able to watch them. By having visual contact you'll be able to manage the belay more effectively, taking in slack in sync with the movement of the climber. Giving advice to a climber who encounters a challenging section may prove ineffective if the instructor can't actually see them.

Vector Pull

If someone just physically can't do a move or is too tired to climb up a tough crux section, some assistance from the belayer may be enough to get them over the impasse. A simple method is the vector pull.

Imagine a rope strung tight across a chasm, anchored on both ends, rigged for a climber to clip in with a pulley to slide across. This is known as a Tyrolean traverse. If the climber weighs 200 pounds and is hanging from the middle of the rope, with an angle slightly less than 180 degrees, the force at each anchor is roughly 1,000 pounds. As the angle approaches 180 degrees, the force on the anchor points increases even more. Less angle, less force. For example, when the angle is relatively narrow (22 degrees or less), the 200-pound climber weights each anchor with only 100 pounds. Let's say the instructor is belaying from the top of the cliff, and the climber is unable to move up past a tough section of the climb. With a tight rope (180-degree angle), by reaching down and pulling perpendicular to the line of the rope, a surprising amount of force can be generated just by creating an angle slightly less than 180 degrees. By pulling on the rope at a right angle, it is like the climber hanging in the middle of the Tyrolean traverse who is generating ten times his bodyweight at the anchor points. This is often enough to boost someone past a move, especially if he is able to assist by climbing.

3:1 Raising System

One reason to use the direct belay technique with an ABD when belaying from the top of the cliff is that it is easily converted to a 3:1 raising system (aka the Z system) in a matter of seconds. For most climbing instructors, the direct belay is always the first choice, providing the anchor is solid, because it allows the instructor to anticipate and prepare for any eventuality, like a quick lowering or raising of the climber. Most instructors use a Grigri, clipped directly to the master point or extended master point (using the climbing rope). To set up a 3:1 raise, follow these steps:

1. Tie a backup knot (overhand loop) on the brake strand side of the Grigri. This allows the

Also known as the Z pulley system, the 3:1 raising system is easy to rig if a Grigri is being used for a direct belay. The Grigri is the ratchet (which locks off when needed to reset), and the friction hitch is the tractor (which moves up and down the field). The distance the rope travels between resets is called the throw.

instructor to go "hands free" and release the brake strand.

2. Tie a friction hitch (prusik or klemheist) on the load strand going down to the climber.

3. Clip the brake strand side of the rope (from the Grigri) to a locking carabiner clipped to the friction hitch and push the friction hitch as far as possible toward the climber.

4. Next, untie the backup knot and pull up on the brake strand side of the rope. For every 3 feet pulled through the GriGri, the load is raised 1 foot. Friction is the enemy in any raising system.

If the rope going to the climber is in contact with a large surface area of rock, the raise will be correspondingly more difficult. A pulley at the friction hitch carabiner reduces friction and makes it easier to pull. Remember, this technique is for assisting a climber, helping them get past a tough spot, not to haul up a severely injured or unconscious climber.

5. When the friction hitch is all the way to the Grigri, reset the friction hitch by sliding it back down toward the climber. The Grigri's built-in ratchet will lock off and hold the load as this is done. Then continue the raise.

A 3:1 assisted raise. With the climber also pulling, there is a tremendous mechanical advantage, making it far easier to raise someone than with a 3:1 raise.

3:1 Assisted Raise

For this method the climber must be close enough that it is possible to throw him a bight of rope. The climber clips the rope into his harness to assist in the raise. Using this system allows both the climber and instructor to work together, and makes it much easier for the instructor to raise the climber.

The steps are as follows:

1. Tie a backup knot (overhand loop) on the brake strand side of the belay device.

2. Toss a bight of rope down to the climber and have him clip it into his belay loop with a locking carabiner. If he already has a locking carabiner on his harness, have him clip that to his belay loop and to the bight of rope. If not, carefully lower the carabiner down. Don't throw it.

3. Identify which strand the climber should pull on by shaking it.

4. Untie the backup knot.

5. The climber pulls down as the instructor pulls up on the brake strand side of the rope. Warn the climber to watch his hands so they are not pinched in the carabiner when pulling.

CHAPTER 14

Fixed Lines

A fixed line is a rope that is literally fixed in one location to provide additional security to climbers, by providing a line that they can be attached to while moving. In an instructional setting, fixed lines provide a means to protect an individual in a group who is required to move over small sections of exposed 2nd, 3rd, or even 4th-class terrain.

Fixed lines should not be employed to protect long sections of exposed or 5th-class terrain. They should only be installed in areas where the likelihood of a fall is relatively low, but where the consequences of a fall are high enough to warrant additional protection. The first line of defense in these areas is that the terrain is easy enough that the student is unlikely to fall. The fixed line is a backup to the student's ability to effectively scramble. If the consequences of a fall are high, a belay is necessary.

Fixed lines usually take time to rig. If possible, place them before the students arrive. If the local ethic doesn't allow for this, then scout the area thoroughly and make a fixed line plan before the instructional day starts.

Following are the steps for fixed line installation:

1. Scout the crag or the approach to the instructional area for exposure and determine where a fixed line is needed.

2. Build an anchor at the top of the crag and clip the end of the rope into the master point with a locking carabiner.

3. Work down through the exposed area, pulling the rope down and placing gear along the way.

At each piece of gear, the fixed line should be clipped in with a loop knot. The rope should *not* run through the carabiners freely. Each section of the rope should be isolated.

Depending on the fixed line's orientation and the terrain, the means by which the line is secured at the beginning varies. A catastrophe knot or a single anchor point may be sufficient. For traverses or anywhere else that an unfixed end could lead to catastrophe, such as an injury or fatality, an anchor system should be used.

There are three ways commonly used to travel on a fixed line. The method chosen is determined by the terrain, the orientation of the rope, and the amount of security desired. The first, and simplest, method is a hand line. As the name implies, the students simply hold the line. In this case the likelihood of a fall is low, and the individual or group simply needs a little bit of additional security.

Second is to use lobster claws. This technique involves girth-hitching two slings to the tie-in point on the climber's harness with a locking carabiner clipped to the end of each sling. The climber clips and locks both carabiners on the fixed line, then moves along the line. The climber bypasses anchor points by clipping past each point with one lobster claw and then the other. This allows the climber to stay attached to the rope at all times

The lobster claw technique is good for exposed traverses, but is not acceptable when the fixed line is in a vertical orientation where a student could fall back to the previous anchor point. Doing so could generate forces exceeding a factor 2 fall.

The third technique, which offers the greatest security, is to use a friction hitch on the fixed line,

A climber using the lobster claw technique to pass an anchor point.

JASON D. MARTIN

which the climber clips into with a lobster claw. A friction hitch offers the most security because it won't allow the climber to fall anywhere if he or she slips (unless the hitch itself slips). If a section requires such tactics, it's a good idea to pre-rig the friction hitches, to allow the climber to smoothly clip in and continue moving. When the climber arrives at a friction hitch, one lobster claw is clipped to the friction hitch and the other to the rope.

The friction hitch fixed line technique should be used sparingly. If you believe that you need to resort to this technique, first ask yourself if it would be possible to belay the section. If you cannot belay the section, then consider the consequences of a friction hitch slipping. If the consequences are high, you may need to choose a different crag. No matter which technique you choose to employ, only one climber should ever be attached to a given part of the line. You should never have two climbers in the same section of the system.

Fixed lines are a useful tool, but they should not take the place of a real belay. Before exposing students to a fixed line, make sure to weigh all the options. Make sure that it is the best solution to the problem. And make sure that everybody knows exactly what they're supposed to do as they move up or down the line.

A climber is using a friction hitch (prusik) on the rope for more security. Note the bight of rope coming down from above. When a piece is not available, it is often possible to use a long bight of rope to extend a less convenient placement in order to continue the logical route of the fixed line.

JASON D. MARTIN

CHAPTER 15

Leading

Leading is dangerous, whether the instructor is on the sharp end with an inexperienced belayer, or watching a student lead for the first time. The risk management mantra of "What is the likelihood of a fall and what are the consequences?" should be in the forefront of the instructor's mind when lead climbing with students.

Student Lead Belay Training

When an instructor works at a venue that requires a lead to access the anchors, it is important to add a lead belay contingent to the belay lesson. Once the PBUS (pull, brake, under, slide) technique has been taught and the student demonstrates proficiency, then it is appropriate for an instructor to move into a lead belay lesson.

The orientation of the student's hands while belaying a leader should reflect the posture taken in the braking position of the PBUS. The student pays out rope with the guide hand above the device, while the brake hand remains in the same position below the device. If the student needs to bring rope back in, he or she simply reverts back to the PBUS toproping technique.

There are instructors who prefer to have students belay them with an assisted braking device. The advantage to these devices is that they reduce the likelihood of catastrophic failure of the system. The problem with them is they are far from foolproof and require specialized instruction and technique.

There are a number of devices on the market, and they all have their own idiosyncrasies. It's important to read all associated instructions before

Patty Kline belays a leader using the principal belay position for the Grigri.

Leading with a Student Belayer

W hen you're leading, you should just assume that you're soloing."

It was my (JDM) first year working as a climbing instructor, and this was one of the first things another young instructor shared with me. At the time it made sense. Indeed, in my first two years of instructing, I led literally hundreds of pitches with terrible student belays.

But then it came to me.

The student belays weren't terrible because the students were inexperienced belayers. The student belays were terrible because I didn't invest the time and energy in the students to ensure that their lead belay technique was flawless. From that time forward, I invested myself in ensuring that my lead belays were solid.

Approximately a year after I started spending more time with students on belay technique, I was teaching an aid-climbing clinic in Red Rock Canyon. I placed a piece behind a massive flake and bounce tested it.

It held.

As I worked my way up to the top of my aiders, the flake shifted and the piece popped. I dropped about 6 feet before the rope arrested my fall. The energy that I put into the belay lesson was not wasted. My student easily caught me.

using a new device, follow the manufacturer's recommendations, heed the manufacturer's warnings, and practice with the device prior to using in an institutional setting.

The Petzl Grigri is one of the more common devices on the market. As a result, lead belay technique with the Grigri is described here.

The primary belaying position for the Grigri is the PBUS position, with a guide hand above the device on the rope and a brake hand below. As a leader moves up the rock, the belayer slowly feeds rope through the device, gently pulling with the guide hand, while pushing rope through with the brake hand. If the rope is fed at an appropriate speed, the cam in the Grigri will not engage.

In this principal belay position, the belayer's brake hand never leaves the rope. If there is a need to bring in slack, the belayer reverts to the PBUS toproping technique.

Because the cam automatically engages with a sudden acceleration of the rope, it can be difficult to pay out slack quickly. The simplest solution to this problem is to never allow the rope to suddenly accelerate. This may be accomplished by the leader placing gear at chest level or lower and extending the protection with runners. Doing so allows the leader to clip into the protection without having to give a quick tug on the rope.

If the curricular goal is to teach a student the finer points of lead belaying, then there are two ways to give slack to a climber who needs it quickly. The first and easiest way is to simply step in toward the wall. This will immediately put slack into the system and works well. However, this technique is not recommended for novice belayers as they are often tied down to ground anchors and cannot easily move.

The second way is to shift the brake hand, sliding it up the rope to the device, and brace the index

The proper way to give slack quickly with a Petzl Grigri.

finger against the lip of the moving sideplate. Press the thumb of the brake hand down on the cam where the handle is attached while continuing to hold the brake strand of the rope. Pull slack with the guide hand. Once finished, immediately return to the principal belay position.

Petzl recommends that you:

1. Always keep the brake strand in the brake hand. There is never a valid reason to let go of the brake strand.

2. Never grip the device with the entire hand.

3. Anticipate the lead climber's movement, including when additional rope is needed to make a clip.

In a toprope setting, a rope is generally set up early in the day and may be used to practice belaying. In a lead setting, practicing this skill requires some creativity. One method is to clip the first bolt of a sport route, or place a piece of gear about 10 feet up. Clip the rope and then have the student practice belaying a leader on this short mock setup.

Ground Anchors, Student Belay Backups, and Knots

In addition to using a Grigri and placing a lot of protection, here are three other ways to increase instructor security during a lead. First, use a ground anchor. Second, employ a backup belayer. And third, tie knots in the rope behind the belayer and the backup belayer.

A ground anchor keeps the belayer under control. The belayer is fixed to a given spot. If the belayer is anchored, the opportunity to trip, fall over, and pull the instructor off is greatly reduced. The belayer will remain in the designated stance.

With two or more students, a backup belayer will increase security. It is far less likely that both students will drop the leader. To add even greater security, put a friction hitch on the rope behind the belayer and attach it to the backup belayer's belay loop. Rather than being dependent on a hand belay, the backup belayer manages the rope with the assistance of a "third hand."

Some instructors tie knots in the rope behind the belayer and the backup belayer. As the instructor leads and the knots approach the belay team, either the backup belayer or, ideally, a third student unties them. Even if there are a series of mistakes, the leader will still have a reasonable margin of error.

No matter what steps are taken to increase instructor security, it remains important to regularly look down and check on the belayer. Make sure that the belay system is employed appropriately and communicate error corrections as needed.

Descent Options

If walking off or downclimbing is not possible for the climbing instructor, the other descent options from the top of a route are either to rappel or be lowered.

The most secure method is to rappel. When being lowered, the instructor is completely reliant on the belay system and at the greatest exposure to risk of system failure. If there are any doubts about the security of the system (i.e., the belayer), the instructor should rappel.

However, if the curricular goal of the program is to teach the student how to operate as an independent climber, then the student will have to learn how to lower. When faced with that situation, the instructor can mitigate the risk by placing a friction hitch on the belay strand of the rope as a backup, clipping the friction hitch to a sling that is then clipped into the instructor's belay loop with a locking carabiner. While being lowered, the instructor manages the friction hitch, releasing it if the belayer loses control of the brake strand.

Teaching a Student to Lead

When teaching lead climbing skills, it is important to know whether or not the organization offering the course permits students to lead. It is also important to find out if the insurance policy permits student leads.

Regardless of whether the organization or insurance policy allows leading, prospective leaders should spend a great deal of time mock leading. A mock leader is a climber who is on toprope while simultaneously dragging a lead line. The toprope protects the student from a real fall, while the lead line provides the illusion of leading. The student can place gear or clip bolts just as if leading for real, but without the consequences.

After a student has completed a mock trad lead, the instructor can climb the route and inspect the pieces. Ideally, the instructor will provide the student with feedback on the quality of each placement while removing the gear.

An instructor may also choose to have a student belay the mock leader while the instructor ascends a fixed line beside the leader, which will allow the instructor to give feedback in the moment. The instructor may use the same rope climbing technique as described for a climber pickoff (chapter 13, Basic Assistance and Rescue Skills).

If only one rope is available, it is still possible to set up a mock lead. Simply tie both ends of the rope into the climber. One end will come from the climber's harness, run up through the toprope anchor, and drop back down to the belayer. The rest of the rope will lay in a pile between the climber and belayer.

The advantage of the single line mock lead system is that only one rope has to be carried. However, there are two disadvantages with a single line. First, students will have to unclip each piece as they are lowered. There won't be enough rope to leave it running through the pieces. And second, with a single line system, the student may have a harder time distinguishing between the belay line and the lead line. When climbers have two ropes in a mock lead scenario, they're usually different colors. This makes it easier for students to distinguish between the lead line and the belay line.

Most instructors will spend a great deal of time in ground school, teaching students how to place gear or clip bolts before moving into a mock lead sequence. Sport leaders should understand how to clip correctly before getting on the rock, while trad leaders should have a solid understanding of gear placement. Both sport climbers and trad climbers need to be educated in placement or clipping strategies before working their skills on a mock lead.

If teaching a clinic on sport leading, be sure to spend significant time in ground school practicing the transition from a toprope to a rappel. This can be done using traditional pieces close to the ground. Clip locking carabiners to two solid pieces and treat them like bolts. The student will then be

A climber mock leads on a single rope. Note the rope running up to the anchor above the climber, back down to the belayer, into the pile on the ground, and then back to the climber.

able to practice the transition from start to finish.

If the instructor is in a position to allow students to lead for real, be extremely conservative. Beginning leaders should not fall. By choosing an appropriate crag—a crag where the student feels confident, or a very easy route, or even a 4th-class route—the exposure to potential student injury decreases dramatically.

Occasionally, an instructor may have a student who is an experienced climber and would like to lead. If organization policy and insurance allow this, then the instructor has to be the one to decide whether or not it's appropriate for the student to lead. This generally requires some assessment of both the student's movement skills and ability to clip or place gear appropriately. If an instructor doesn't like what he or she sees in a student assessment, then the instructor should not be afraid to say no. It's better to have an upset student than a seriously injured student.

Appendix A:
Leave No Trace Ethics

Climbers should practice Leave No Trace principles from the moment they step out of the car. The following simple steps will help keep the climbing sites we all share as clean as possible, with minimal degradation to the climbing area and the surrounding environment:

- At popular climbing areas, use the outhouses located at most parking areas before you embark on your approach to that day's chosen cliff.

- Always use marked climber's access trails where they are available. If there is no marked trail to the cliff, minimize your impact by walking on durable surfaces (e.g., a sandy wash, rock slab, or barren ground).

- At popular, easy-access crags, avoid making a beeline from the parking lot straight to the crag without first looking for an established path or trail. Walking off-trail can significantly impact vegetation and cause soil erosion if enough people do it over a period of time.

- If traveling in a group in more remote, pristine areas where no trail exists, fan out instead of walking in single file and try to walk on the most durable surfaces, avoiding fragile vegetation. Don't leave rock cairns to mark the path, as this takes away the challenge of routefinding from those who prefer to experience it on their own terms.

- If nature calls and you're far from any outhouse, deposit solid human waste well away from the base of any climbing site, water source, or wash by digging a cathole 4 to 6 inches deep. Cover and disguise the cathole when you're done. Pack out all toilet paper and tampons in a ziplock bag. Better yet, use "blue bags" and pack out all human waste. Urinate on bare ground or rock, not plants. Urine contains salt, and animals will dig into plants to get at it.

- Leave no trace means just that—pack out everything you bring in, including all trash and food waste (that means apple cores and orange peels, too). Set an example for your group by picking up any trash you find; plan ahead and always carry a trash bag with you when you go out to the crag.

Principles of Leave No Trace

1. Plan ahead and prepare
2. Travel and camp on durable surfaces
3. Dispose of waste properly
4. Leave what you find
5. Minimize campfire impacts
6. Respect wildlife
7. Be considerate of other visitors

- Don't monopolize popular routes by setting up a toprope and then leaving your rope hanging on the climb, unused. If your climb begins from a campsite, ask permission to climb from the campers if the site is occupied. Minimize your use of chalk, and if you're working a route, clean off any tic marks with a soft brush after you're done. Protect everyone's access to a climbing area by being courteous, beginning with parking only in designated areas and carpooling whenever possible. Noise pollution can be a problem, from blasting tunes on a boom box to yelling and screaming while attempting a hard climb. Be considerate and aware of those around you, and limit your noise production to a reasonable level.

- Pick up all food crumbs and don't feed any wild critters—this habituates them to human food and encourages them to beg and scavenge, sometimes even chewing holes in backpacks to get at food.

- Leave all natural and cultural objects so that they can be experienced by everyone in their natural setting. If you are climbing in a national forest or national park, obey all regulations concerning the gathering of firewood and other objects.

For more information on Leave No Trace ethics, visit www.LNT.org.

Appendix B:
How to Determine a Fall Factor

Fall factors are determined by a simple formula. Divide the length of the fall by the length of rope out between the belayer and climber.

The greater the fall factor, the greater the force on the rope, on the belayer, and on the anchor. A factor 2 fall is the maximum that may be attained in a standard climbing fall, since the length of a fall can't exceed twice the length of the rope.

In a multi-pitch setting, a factor 2 fall only takes place when a leader who has not placed any protection takes an unobstructed fall, drops past the belayer, and then falls directly onto the belayer's system. If the climber places protection above the belayer, it is no longer possible to generate a factor 2 fall, as the length of the fall can no longer be twice the length of the rope out.

Many other factors play into the calculation of a true fall factor. For example, if an individual tumbles down a slab, the impact will be quite different than if he fell unobstructed. If the belayer is pulled off the ground or a piece fails, all of these things change the true math.

A factor 2 fall is extremely serious. The forces generated can exceed the strength rating of gear, potentially resulting in anchor failure. Also, the impact force on the belayer is tremendous. Loss of control of the belay or injury to the belayer are both possible outcomes. As such, it is imperative

Fall Factors

Following are some simple word problems that you can use to determine if you understand how to calculate fall factors:

1. A lead climber places a piece 15 feet off a belay. As he reaches 20 feet, he falls, dropping 10 feet. What type of fall factor did he generate?

2. A lead climber on a multi-pitch climb leads 50 feet up above his belayer without placing any gear. He slips and drops 50 feet back to his belayer and then continues to fall another 50 feet, for a grand total of 100 feet. What type of fall factor did he generate?

3. A lead climber is 50 feet up. His last piece is 10 feet below him. He falls. What kind of fall factor did he generate?

Answers: (1) Factor 0.5, (2) Factor 2, (3) Factor 0.4

that multi-pitch climbers use the anchor as the first piece of protection or place gear immediately after leaving the belay station. This will limit the possibility of a high-impact fall.

Single Pitch Instructors are not as concerned about fall factors as much as multi-pitch guides, but there is still cause for concern.

A common practice among climbers is to clip into the anchor with a personal tether. Personal tethers include slings, a PAS, or a daisy chain. If the climber is positioned above the anchor, clipped in with a personal tether, and falls, a high-impact fall—potentially as high as a factor 2 fall—will occur. Due to the static nature of tether material, there is a possibility that the personal tether will break. Some tether materials, like nylon, do better in testing than others, but a fall onto a tether is still a concern that has to be kept in mind. Additionally, the impact force generated to the climber's body can easily result in an injury. The takeaway point here is that a climber does not need to be tied into a rope to suffer a factor 2 fall.

Calculating the fall factor.

MIKE CLELLAND

Appendix C:
Autoblocking Devices

Autoblocking devices like the Petzl Reverso, the Black Diamond ATC Guide, the Mammut Bionic Alpine, the CAMP PIU 2, and the myriad of others on the market are not covered in the Single Pitch Instructor curriculum. These devices are excellent multi-pitch devices and work well in a single pitch environment. However, many new instructors come into the AMGA Single Pitch Instructor Course with limited experience working with assisted braking devices and the Munter hitch. It is extremely important for instructors to understand how to use these tools, since they are the best tools for Single Pitch Instructor terrain. Students who move into the upper-level AMGA courses spend a great deal of time working with autoblocking devices, but at the beginner level, instructors must first have a baseline understanding of essential tools.

Though autoblocking devices are not part of the curriculum and candidates will not be tested on them, it was felt that they should be covered in this text. This is primarily because autoblocking devices are increasingly common at both single and multi-pitch crags throughout the country, and most students have been exposed to them.

Autoblocking devices are a hybrid between standard tube-style devices and plaquette-style devices. They can be used to belay a leader or to toprope, just like any other tube-style device. However, they have one additional feature. When belaying from above, they can be hung directly from the anchor by an additional carabiner hole and rigged to securely belay one or two climbers.

As with all climbing equipment, it's important

An autoblocking device set up in "guide mode," loaded with the climber strand on the top and the belay strand on the bottom.

to read the manufacturer's instructions. These devices vary and there are small differences between them. But the concept is the same. A bight of rope runs through the vertical slot on the front of the device, with the strand on top going to the climber and the belay strand on the bottom. This bight is secured to the back of the device with a locking carabiner. When weighted, the strand going to the climber squeezes the belay line, holding it in position and locking it off.

If these devices are loaded improperly, the autoblocking function will not engage. Always pull down on the climber's line after loading the device to ensure that it locks. If the climber's line moves easily, the device is not loaded properly.

Another reason this device is not taught in the SPI curriculum is that, when set up in autoblocking mode, it requires specialized techniques to unlock the device when it is loaded. It is important to understand that these devices, when in autoblock mode, were not designed for long lowers and are a poor choice for lowering a climber in single pitch terrain. Situations may arise that require unlocking an autoblocking device to lower a climber a short distance, and users should understand how that can be accomplished. Following are three methods.

Simple Lower by Ratcheting Carabiner

The first type of lower requires that a belayer crank the locking carabiner that secures the bight of rope back and forth. This allows the load to lower incrementally. This method is used for very short lowers. It is important for the belayer to keep the brake hand on the brake strand of the rope during this process.

Simple Lower with a Nut Tool or Carabiner

In the second lower, a nut tool or small carabiner is used to leverage the device. This method works well for lowers of one or two body lengths. Following is a breakdown of the lower:

A belayer ratchets the carabiner up and down to complete a short lower.

JASON D. MARTIN

1. Attach a friction hitch to the brake strand and clip it to the belayer's belay loop.

2. Put a nut tool or carabiner in the small hole in the bottom of the autoblocking device.

3. Crank the device up and back, "breaking" the autoblock's hold on the rope.

4. Maintain control of the brake strand while allowing the rope to pass slowly through the device.

5. Once the lower is complete, return the device to its original position.

Using a carabiner to open up the device in order to make a short lower.

Complex Lower with a Redirect

This method can be used for moderate-length lowers. Again, if a longer lower is required, the system should be transferred to a more secure system. Following is a breakdown of the lower.

1. Tie off the backside of the rope with a catastrophe knot.
2. Attach a friction hitch to the brake strand and clip it to the belayer's belay loop.
3. Place a carabiner somewhere high in the anchor system, above the autoblocking device.
4. Redirect the brake strand through the carabiner high in the system.
5. Run a cord or a sling through the small hole in the bottom of the autoblocking device.
6. Thread the cord or sling through a second carabiner high in the system and attach it to the belayer's belay loop.
7. Untie the catastrophe knot.
8. Lean back on the redirected cord, "breaking" the system.
9. Maintain control of the brake strand while allowing the rope to pass slowly through the device.
10. Once the lower is complete, return the device to its original position.

Appendix D: Wilderness Medical Certifications

AMGA Single Pitch Instructors are required to hold and maintain a Wilderness First Aid (WFA) certificate if they intend to work in the frontcountry, or a Wilderness First Responder (WFR) certificate if they intend to work in the backcountry. If it will take you less than 2 hours to evacuate a student to definitive medical care, then you are working in the frontcountry. However, if it will take more than 2 hours, then you are working in the backcountry and you will need to hold a WFR certification.

A number of organizations throughout the United States offer WFA and WFR certifications, though not all certifications are the same. Some require recertification every two years, while others require it every three. Some companies have reciprocity with one another, while others do not. Be sure to do your research before committing to a certification course. You should know what you're getting into ahead of time and should be aware of how easy—or how hard—it will be to find recertification courses when your certification expires.

In addition to a WFA or WFR certification, instructors are required to hold and maintain a CPR certification.

Following is a breakdown of common wilderness first-aid medical certifications.

Wilderness First Aid (WFA)

This 16- to 30-hour program provides a baseline introduction to wilderness medicine. This course is recognized by the AMGA as a minimum requirement for individuals working in a frontcountry environment.

Wilderness First Responder (WFR)

This 70- to 90-hour certification course is considered a baseline requirement for most backcountry professionals in the United States. The AMGA recognizes this as a minimum level of training for those working in a backcountry wilderness environment.

Outdoor Emergency Care (OEC)

The National Ski Patrol developed the OEC as a first-aid program for members of the ski patrol who work at resorts. This program requires students to devote 80 to 100 hours to the course of study. The AMGA recognizes this as an equivalency to the Wilderness First Responder, as do many land managers.

Wilderness Emergency Medical Technician (WEMT)

The WEMT course meets all the requirements of an EMT course as well as the requirements of a WFR course. Most programs require four weeks of full-time intensive study. The AMGA recognizes this as a higher level of training than the WFR program.

Appendix E:
Recommended Reading

Climbing instructors should have a strong understanding of the contents of a wide array of instructional climbing texts. The following are excellent resources for the Single Pitch Instructor candidate. The seasoned certified instructor may find these texts useful to supplement lessons.

Baseline Climbing Skills

Climbing Anchors. John Long and Bob Gaines. Globe Pequot Press/FalconGuides. Guilford, CT. 2013.

Rock Climbing Anchors: A Comprehensive Guide. Craig Luebben. The Mountaineers Books. Seattle, WA. 2007.

Rock Climbing: Mastering the Basic Skills. Craig Luebben. The Mountaineers Books. Seattle, WA. 2004.

Toproping. Bob Gaines. Globe Pequot Press/ FalconGuides. Guilford, CT. 2012.

Rappelling. Bob Gaines. Globe Pequot Press/ FalconGuides. Guilford, CT. 2013.

Advanced Climbing and Instructional Skills

Coaching Climbing. Michelle Hurni. Globe Pequot Press. Guilford, CT. 2002.

The Rock Warrior's Way: Mental Training for Climbers. Arno Ilgner. Desiderata Institute. La Vergne, TN. 2006.

Self Rescue, 2nd ed. David Fasulo. Globe Pequot Press/FalconGuides. Guilford, CT. 2011.

Technical Handbook for Professional Mountain Guides. American Mountain Guides Association. Boulder, CO. 1998.

Adventure Activities / Outdoor Leadership / Education

The Backcountry Classroom: Lessons, Tools and Activities for Teaching Outdoor Leaders. Jack Drury, Bruce Bonney, Dene Berman, and Mark Wagstaff. ICS Books. Merrillville, IN. 1992.

Best New Games. Dale N. LeFevre. Human Kinetics. Champagne, IL. 2002.

Cowstails and Cobras II: A Guide to Games, Initiatives, Ropes Courses & Adventure Curriculum. Karl Rohnke. Project Adventure, Inc. Hamilton, MA. 1998.

Islands of Healing: A Guide to Adventure Based Counseling. Jim Schoel, Dick Prouty, and Paul Radcliffe. Project Adventure. Beverly, MA. 1989.

Outdoor Leadership: Techniques, Common Sense and Self-Confidence. John Graham. The Mountaineers Books. Seattle, WA. 1997.

Soft Paths. David Cole, Bruce Hampton, and Dana Watts. Stackpole Books. Harrisburg, PA. 1998.

Appendix F: Climbing Instructor Employment Resources

The following resources may be helpful when searching for a job in the outdoor industry. Many of these provide a variety of job opportunities for outdoor educators, instructors, and guides, so pay close attention to find the job that is the right fit.

AMGA Newsletter

www.amga.com

After completing the AMGA Single Pitch Instructor Course, members will be placed on the American Mountain Guides Association mailing and e-mail lists. The AMGA's monthly newsletter includes listings for mountain guide and climbing instructor jobs.

The AMGA job board tends to lean heavily toward for-profit guide services.

AORE Listserv

www.aore.org

The Association of Outdoor Recreation and Education was designed to bring together outdoor professionals in college recreation and outdoor pursuits programs and community and military recreation programs for an annual conference. The yearly conference was designed for academic outdoor professionals to network and trade ideas.

AORE members have access to a listserv that has an academic focus, and many of the jobs are at universities or community colleges.

There is an annual fee to become a member of the AORE community.

Association for Experiential Education

www.aee.org

This is another association that has an academic focus. Like the AORE job announcements, this organization posts a wide array of jobs, from those at schools, to challenge courses, to climbing walls.

Backdoor Jobs

www.backdoorjobs.com/ adventure.html

The Backdoor Jobs website is devoted to adventure tourism jobs including climbing and mountaineering, but also covers rafting, backpacking, and mountain biking guides.

Certified Guides Co-op

www.certifiedguidescooperative.com

The Certified Guides Co-op provides Single Pitch Instructors with significant professional work history an opportunity to gain access and insurance. The Co-op is designed for instructors with an established client base who wish to work independently of a guide service, school, or other organization. Instructors must have at least 200 days of single pitch instruction after they become certified instructors to apply.

Chronicle of Higher Education

www.chronicle.com

This is a university job board that focuses heavily on academic jobs.

Military Recreation Jobs

www.armymwr.com;
www.navymwr.org;
www.nafjobs.org;
www.usajobs.gov

As the military is extremely broad, so are the job resources. These are a select few websites where you may find outdoor recreation job opportunities on and around military bases.

Mountain Guide Jobs

www.mountainguidejobs.com

This is a site that provides a very short list of organizations and companies that are looking for climbing and mountaineering guides.

NOLS Jobs Announcements

www.nols.edu/alumni/contact/listservices.php

The NOLS Jobs Announcements is a listserv designed for outdoor professionals. It provides information on some NOLS-related jobs, but the majority of the listings are for adventure education jobs throughout the United States and Canada.

This listserv was designed with NOLS and Wilderness Medicine Institute alumni in mind. However, it does not discriminate against those who have not taken a NOLS course.

This is an extremely active job board, with dozens of new postings coming through every week.

Outdoor Adventure Professional Network

http://adventurejobs.co/

This particular site posts jobs in all the outdoor disciplines.

Outdoor Ed

www.outdoored.com

The Outdoor Ed website is a job-listing website that provides information on both seasonal and year-round adventure tourism jobs. Mountaineering and rock instruction jobs are regularly highlighted on the site.

Outdoor Industry Jobs

www.outdoorindustryjobs.com

This website is a dumping ground of outdoor industry–related jobs. There are some adventure educator and guide jobs on the site, but many of the jobs are retail and gear representation.

Rock Climbing Jobs

www.rockclimbingjobs.com

This site focuses on rock climbing jobs at adventure summer camps.

Northwest Information Exchange

http://groups.google.com/group/nw-information-exchange?pli=1

The Northwest Information Exchange is a place where instructors and guides in the Pacific Northwest trade information about current conditions in the mountains. However, guide service owners and staffing managers regularly post open positions on the listserv.

You will need to be actively working as a guide or instructor for a guide service to get access to the listserv.

San Juan Information Exchange

https://groups.google.com/ forum/?hl=en-US#!forum/ San-Juan-information-exchange

This is a guide conditions listserv like the Northwest Information Exchange. However, the focus of this exchange is the Ouray/Telluride/ Silverton/Durango area of Colorado. Occasionally employment requests are sent out through the listserv.

Like the Northwest Exchange, you must be actively working in the field for a guide service to obtain access to the site.

Index

About the Authors

Bob Gaines began rock climbing at Joshua Tree in the 1970s. Since then he has pioneered over 400 first ascents in the park. Bob began his career as a professional rock climbing guide in 1983 and is the owner of Vertical Adventures Rock Climbing School, which offers classes and guided climbs at Joshua Tree. In 2008 Vertical Adventures was voted the number 1 rock climbing school in America by *Outside* magazine.

Bob has worked extensively in the film business as a climbing stunt coordinator. He has coordinated over forty television commercials, and he was Sylvester Stallone's climbing instructor for the movie *Cliffhanger.* Bob is an AMGA Certified Rock Climbing Instructor and currently teaches the AMGA Single Pitch Instructor Course at Joshua Tree. He has worked extensively training US military special forces, including US Navy Seal Team 6, and is known for his technical expertise in anchoring and rescue techniques.

Bob is also the author of *Best Climbs Joshua Tree, Best Climbs Tahquitz and Suicide Rocks, Toproping, Rappelling,* and the co-author of *Climbing Anchors* (with John Long).

Jason D. Martin is an AMGA Certified Rock Guide, the operations director at the American Alpine Institute, and a freelance writer. He has been teaching the AMGA Single Pitch Instructor Course since the program's inception in 2008. Much of Jason's adventure writing revolves around the work he does in the mountains. Jason has professionally guided in the Cascades, the Sierra, Red Rock Canyon, Joshua Tree National Park, the Alaska Range, the Coast Mountains of Canada, and in the Andes of Bolivia, Ecuador, and Peru. He wrote the guidebook *Fun Climbs Red Rocks: Topropes and Moderates* and co-authored *Washington Ice: A Climbing Guide.* His writing has appeared in the *Seattle Post Intelligencer, San Antonio Current, Mt. Baker Experience, Northwest Mountaineering Journal, Climbing* magazine, and in numerous other publications. He currently manages the American Alpine Institute blog (blog .alpineinstitute.com), generating numerous climbing and outdoor articles every week. In addition to his work as an outdoor writer and guide, Jason is also a playwright and film critic.

FIND A GUIDE » BECOME ONE

AMERICAN MOUNTAIN GUIDES ASSOCIATION

1979

AMGA.COM